Strategies for the Threshold #2

Dealing with Ziz: Spirit of Forgetting

Anne Hamilton

Dealing with Ziz: Spirit of Forgetting
Strategies for the Threshold #2

Published by Armour Books
P. O. Box 492, Corinda QLD 4075

Cover Image: © Steve Creitz / GoodSalt.com
Section Divider Image: © Can Stock Photo / lachshi
Interior Design and Typeset by Book Whispers

ISBN: 978-1-925380-12-5

A catalogue record for this book is available from the National Library of Australia

Strategies for the Threshold #2

Dealing with Ziz: Spirit of Forgetting

Anne Hamilton

Other Books By
Anne Hamilton

In this series

Dealing with Python: Spirit of Constriction

Devotional Theology

God's Poetry: The Identity & Destiny Encoded in Your Name
God's Panoply: The Armour of God & the Kiss of Heaven
God's Pageantry: The Threshold Guardians & the Covenant Defender
God's Pottery: The Sea of Names & the Pierced Inheritance
God's Priority: World-Mending & Generational Testing
More Precious than Pearls:
The Mother's Blessing & God's Favour Towards Women
(with *Natalie Tensen*)

Mathematics and Theology in Medieval Poetry

Gawain and the Four Daughters of God:
the testimony of mathematics in Cotton Nero A.x

Award-winning Children's Books

Many-Coloured Realm
Daystar: The Days are Numbered Book 1
Merlin's Wood: The Battle of the Trees 1

Contents

Introduction		ix
1	**Keepers of Memory**	1
2	**Remember, Remember**	21
3	**Bridge of Birds**	39
4	**The Mezuzah of God**	73
5	**The Hill of Government**	93
6	**Watchkeeper Bride**	133
7	**Through All Generations**	169
Appendix 1	**Brief Summary**	185
Appendix 2	**Common Symbols of Ziz**	189
Appendix 3	**Governing Vows**	190
Appendix 4	**Complicity and Salvation**	192
Appendix 5	**Geography**	195
Endnotes		199

Introduction

For months, my neck had been so stiff and tight I could hardly move it. When I wanted to look back over my shoulder, I had to turn my whole body rather than just my head. I was driving home from work late one afternoon when a bubble of thought broke the surface of my conscious mind: 'You know, this might just be a spiritual problem.'

So I prayed. It wasn't very elaborate or refined. It was just a simple request. I don't think I even attached 'amen' or 'in Jesus' name'. It went something like this: 'Father, if this is a spiritual problem, would You please tell the spirit to go away.'

Nothing happened for about five minutes. Then I felt as if a thick rope with several giant knots in it was being pulled out of my spine through my neck. After several excruciating jerks, all was well. I could move my neck easily in any direction. I thanked God and thought very little more about it.

Some time later, the neck problem returned. If I'd known what I know now about neck issues and the spirit of Python, I would have realised that was a very likely outcome. As soon as another significant decision was approaching, it was unavoidable. I put up with the stiff neck for several weeks before—*suddenly*—I remembered that the last time this had happened it had been a spiritual problem. So, again, I turned to the Lord and prayed very simply. And again, the 'rope' with the giant knots in it came out of my neck in excruciating jerks.

As troubling as the neck pain was, I became far more concerned about my memory. How could I forget the cause of the problem was spiritual? It didn't seem the sort of thing I was ever likely to forget. It didn't immediately dawn on me there was a spirit of forgetting who was more cunning than I could possibly dream of. In retrospect, it should have.

This book is about that spirit.

It is, of course, not the last word on the subject. Like my other books, it's the beginning of a dialogue, an opening-up of a topic long overlooked. Forgotten, in fact.

And like all my other books, it's got a numerical underlay. Each chapter is divided into sections and most of them are multiples of 111—the covenant number found in the mathematical structure of John 17—as well as the odd sprinkling of the golden ratio—taken from the pattern in Genesis 1:1.

My thanks to my mum, who once again has written some beautiful prayers for the end of each chapter. Heartfelt thanks also to Janice, Janette, Donna and Alison for their insightful comments on the raw manuscript. I pray that, as you read, the Father of our Lord Jesus Christ will overshadow you with His protection. I pray too that nothing written here in any way constitutes an invitation for the spirits named to be present as you progress through the book—but instead the words will dispel any mind-fog you've experienced through their activity in your life. May you grow in wisdom to discern the wiles of the evil one and never let go of the hem of Jesus' garment as He arises on your life with healing in His wings.

Anne Hamilton

Brisbane, Australia 2018

1

Keepers of Memory

I'd spent the morning looking at paintings of biblical landscapes in the hope I'd find the 'perfect' cover for a book. However I had become so absorbed in some of the symbolism and detail that I'd actually forgotten to jot down the artists' names or their websites. That's how this discovery started. It's entirely and eminently appropriate it should have begun as a result of an episode of forgetting.

In trying to retrace my steps, I bumbled into the Fine Art America website. There I came across an unusual, abstract painting by Naomi Jacobs. It wasn't my style but it grabbed my attention with its off-beat, memorable title: *Few Knew That Leviathan Helped Shape The Nile Cataracts Started An Impressive Swimmingpool Business.*

Embedded in that curious and awkward description was a revelation: Leviathan was associated with the waterfalls of the Nile River. Now despite many investigations into Leviathan I had never uncovered even the vaguest hint of such a connection. So off I went, delving into this new line of research. Five minutes later, I found the name of a spirit I'd never previously encountered.

Ziz.

At first, I was tempted to dismiss it. The whole description was far too fantastic to be in any way credible. Like Leviathan, this colossal creature was said to be associated with eclipses. Ziz was conceptualised as a giant griffin-like bird with vast wings that could cover the sky from one side to the other. As I read on, I decided that Ziz was a legendary monster, mentioned only rarely in rabbinical folklore. It was, I felt, something I could safely ignore.

I was just about to get back to my search for the perfect cover, when the article on Ziz mentioned that it appears two, perhaps three, times in the Bible. I was taken aback. Seriously aback. Python after all is only ever explicitly mentioned *once* in Scripture—but that doesn't mean to say that's its sole appearance. *Two* or *three* references!? This meant I couldn't just dismiss Ziz as an irrelevant myth. I decided to check it out. Very quickly I realised that a whole jigsaw of seemingly unrelated information I'd come across over many years slotted neatly into the enigma of Ziz.

Ziz is found twice in the Hebrew of Psalms and perhaps also in Isaiah's prophecy. However, these appearances are invariably obscured in translation. A brief look at several related words nevertheless revealed Ziz as a threshold spirit I'd encountered many times before under another name: the spirit of forgetting.

This spirit has always been my nominee for Hell's Most Efficient Employee.

And know what? Yep. You've probably guessed already. I'd seriously underestimated it.

To introduce Ziz, I'd like to begin with a brief portion of its legend. Not because I think it's particularly accurate or even instructive, but because the background will give us a feel for how Jewish sages thought about it. Louis Ginzberg in *Legends of the Jews* says:

> *Just as Leviathan is the king of fishes, so the Ziz is appointed to rule over the birds. His name comes from the variety of tastes his flesh has; it tastes like this, zeh, and like that, zeh. The Ziz is as monstrous of size as Leviathan himself. His ankles rest on the earth, and his head reaches to the very sky.*
>
> *It once happened that travellers on a vessel noticed a bird. As he stood in the water, it merely covered his feet, and his head knocked against the sky. The onlookers thought the water could not have any depth at that point, and they prepared to take a bath there. A heavenly voice warned them: 'Alight not here! Once a carpenter's axe slipped from his hand at this spot, and it took it seven years to touch bottom.'*
>
> *The bird the travellers saw was none other than the Ziz. His wings are so huge that unfurled they darken the sun. They protect the earth against the storms of the south; without their aid the earth would not be able to resist the winds blowing thence.*
>
> *Once an egg of the Ziz fell to the ground and broke. The fluid from it flooded sixty cities,*

and the shock crushed three hundred cedars. Fortunately such accidents do not occur frequently. As a rule the bird lets her eggs slide gently into her nest. This one mishap was because the egg was rotten, and the bird cast it away carelessly.

The Ziz has another name, Renanin, because he is the celestial singer. On account of his relation to the heavenly regions he is also called Sekwi, the seer. Like Leviathan, Ziz is a delicacy to be served to the pious at the end of time.

So, from the legend we learn: the Ziz was conceived of as big. Really big. Big enough to block out the sun and cause eclipses if it were to spread its wings. It was thought to be a mother bird with a strong protective streak. It cared for its eggs; it guarded the earth from the violent dust storms of the southern desert and it even warned occasional travellers of danger.

Its name has an exceedingly dubious etymology, supposedly from the so-so taste of its flesh. A dinner of Ziz awaits the faithful at the banquet which will culminate the present age.

If you've been around my books for any length of time, you'll know how important I think names are. I consider that the meanings of names and, even more importantly, the poetry that surrounds them are the true power behind the purpose of our lives. I believe that the rhymes and wordgames it's possible to play with names can affect both our calling and identity in both positive and negative ways. As I look at Scripture, I am repeatedly astonished to find that God is a wordsmith who delights in crafting new beginnings for people through tweaking and altering names.

So personally, I would have been very grateful for a satisfactory etymology of the name Ziz. It would have been a very helpful starting point when it came to identifying both the function and the nature of the spirit. See, I don't for one solitary second believe the name comes from the bland taste of ziz meat. That explanation sounds just like the sort of answer an exasperated parent would use to fob off a persistent child: 'But why's it called "Ziz", daddy? Why? Why?'

Way back in *God's Poetry*, I made a comment on the following quote from Richard Feynmann—'*You can know the name of a bird in all the languages of the world but when you're finished you'll know absolutely nothing whatsoever about the bird.'* I went on to say that I thought Feynmann was wholly mistaken.

In retrospect perhaps I should have kept that view to myself. If I'd realised I might be setting myself up, I'd have been more careful. I never suspected until very recently that I'd ever be called on to prove my assertion was actually possible. It simply didn't dawn on me that one day I'd be called to back up my disagreement by actually identifying a 'bird', starting with virtually no reliable information other than its name.

To begin to put together the jigsaw that will identify Ziz as the spirit of forgetting—and much more beside—let's begin with Psalm 50:11.

Now an important point to consider regarding forgetting is this: English preserves a unique spiritual understanding of the nature of remembrance. While *forgetting* really is the opposite of *remembering,* it would be vastly more accurate to say that the opposite of *remember* is *dismember. Forgetting* is actually about *dismembering.* And, in presiding over forgetting, the spirit of Ziz has fragmented even the memory of itself. It's difficult to find all the evidence but we can piece together much of what lies hidden and reconstruct and ancient understanding of its nature.

Psalm 50:11 features the first appearance of Ziz in Scriptural Hebrew—'*I know all the birds of the mountains* and Zīz śāday וזיז שדי *is mine.'*

Now it's important to note this verse doesn't actually identify Ziz as a bird. However the clues are there as to how the tradition of a fabulous winged griffin came about. The verse starts with a mention of birds wheeling in flight above the hill country of Israel. It's easy to imagine Asaph, the composer of the song, lifting his eyes higher and allowing his thoughts to transition from the physical world to the spiritual realms—from eagles hovering in the air to marvellous feathered monsters whose heads clipped the stratosphere.

However, English translators have never offered us the possibility that Asaph had this in mind, despite the rabbinic tradition. 'Ziz' in the phrase, 'Zīz śāday', is never rendered as *bird*. Rather it is variously translated as 'insects', 'animals', 'wild beasts', 'everything that moves', 'living things', 'creatures', 'scampering mice' and, in rare dissension, 'beauty' from the Douay-Rheims translation.

Birds don't even rate a passing nod as a possible option.

Now, I'm big on context. But creating an even greater difficulty is the descriptor for this mysterious Ziz: 'śāday'. While it doesn't look like it at first glance, it is in fact the same Hebrew word as 'shaddai'—memorable because it's the very first name God explicitly self-reveals in Scripture.

'Shaddai' first appears in Genesis 17:1 during a name covenant between God and His servant, Abraham.

Eleven years after Abram left Haran for Canaan, God cut a blood covenant with him while he was asleep. Thirteen years along from that incredible moment, God appeared and revealed a previously unknown name: *'I am El-Shaddai—"God Almighty." Serve Me faithfully and live a blameless life.'* (Genesis 17:1 NLT)

God not only disclosed to Abram the secret name, El Shaddai, but He also gave him a new name: Abraham. Now tradition seems to dictate that 'shaddai' be almost universally translated into English as *almighty*. As it transpires, that's not even remotely literal in interpretation. For me at least, *almighty* evokes an image of an iron-strong arm, rock-solid muscles and powerful, protective strength. Such a picture is unfortunate because the actual overtones are a God of warm reassurance, nurturing comfort and close-held tenderness. The root meaning of 'Shaddai' is basically *the strong-breasted one*; it's a maternal image, not a paternal one.

So, to be consistent with this common translation, 'Zīz śāday' perhaps should be rendered as *Ziz almighty*. However that's clearly not the intent of the passage. I suspect it is supposed to be much the same as the Shaddai of God's name—with its overtones of abundance, nourishment and cherishing support.

One reason for thinking this is that, amongst the other unusual features of Psalm 50, it finishes with one of the rarer names of God: Eloah. This is the singular form of the plural Elohim and it is grammatically feminine, in contrast to the masculine of that plural. The psalm actually uses both linguistic forms—at the very beginning, it calls on God as 'El Elohim Yahweh', a title translated as *the Mighty One, God, the Lord*. This particular phrasing is only found elsewhere in Joshua 22:22 during the swearing of an oath concerning remembrance.

The twelve tribes of Israel were physically divided by the Jordan Valley. The people of Gad, Reuben and half the tribe of Manasseh asked permission to settle east of the river. They were granted this right, provided they helped the remainder of the tribal brotherhood conquer the land of Canaan to the west. Faithfully fulfilling this obligation—over a period of seven years—they were then blessed by Joshua and sent home to their families.

But, almost at once, an appalling rumour circulated: it was said that, as the warriors of Gad, Reuben and Manasseh reached Geliloth,[1] they built an altar to another god. Setting off in hot pursuit and ready to war against the very people who'd just helped them achieve their own dream, the tribes of the west demanded an explanation.[2] They reminded the warriors of the east how the whole community had suffered as a result of rebellion in the past—mentioning, first and foremost, the disastrous plague that had come out of the sin of worshipping Peor.

'El Elohim Yahweh! El Elohim Yahweh! He knows!' exclaimed the men of Gad, Reuben and Manasseh as they protested their innocence. They explained it was not an altar to a god other than Yahweh; rather it was an altar that was to serve as a memorial for all generations to come. The name of the altar was *A Witness Between Us—that the Lord is God*. It was built with forethought to the future: if ever the tribes of the west sought to exclude the tribes of the east from worshipping at the Tabernacle and said, 'You have no share in the Lord,' then the altar itself would witness against them.

Now, of course, this explanation quickly resolved the situation and a civil war was averted.

The phrase 'El Elohim Yahweh' remained unique to the Book of Joshua for over half a millennium. It was associated with a monument exhorting the Israelites to remember that Yahweh is El Elohim.

It's about calling to mind who God is.

In Psalm 50, Asaph speaks of God summoning heaven and earth as His witnesses against His people. They have not only forgotten who He is, they have forgotten He will judge them: '*Consider this, you who forget God, or I will tear you to pieces with no one to rescue you...'* (Psalm 50:22 NIV)

'I will tear you to pieces' seems a drastic judgment but it reflects the exact nature of *forgetting*; the opposite of *remembering* is after all *dismembering*.

God's law is: we reap what we sow. So if we forget God—if we dismember His truth—this law means we are subject to precisely the same ruling: to be torn apart. Harsh as it may seem, it is merely our own judgment on ourselves.

This equivalence between forgetting and dismembering recurs time and again throughout Scripture. However, the link is not always obvious on the surface, so there will be times we will have to dig for it.

Take, for example, the Greek word 'alétheia', *truth*. In Ephesians 6:14, Paul encourages his readers to stand firm with the belt of *truth* buckled around their waist. This truth, 'alétheia', is *not forgetting*. The word 'alétheia' is composed of the prefix 'a-', meaning *not*, and 'lethe', the Greek name of the spirit of *forgetfulness, oblivion* and *concealment*.[3] By choosing this particular word, 'alétheia', Paul exhorts us to stand firm against an enemy intent on rending truth apart and consigning the fragments into a shadowy coma.

Before we uncover an alignment between the Greek and Hebrew concepts of forgetting, let's return to Ziz. Thirty chapters after its first appearance in the Book of Psalms, it turns up for the second time. Jewish folklore classes this as its final appearance; however, a brief search of a concordance turns up a third possibility in Isaiah.

Perhaps not altogether surprisingly, the second appearance of Ziz occurs in another song by Asaph. This Levitical musician left a treasure trove of information about threshold guardians in his compositions: as just one example, in Psalm 74, another of his songs, there occurs one of the very rare comments on Leviathan, the spirit of backlash and ally of Ziz. In that psalm the people[4] are said to feed on Leviathan; but the opposite is true when it comes to Ziz in Psalm 80. There the people of Israel are torn apart by this entity and consumed. Psalm 80:13 says: '*The boar from the forest ravages it, and* Zīz śāday זיז שדי *feeds on it.*'

In this song, the people of Israel are envisaged as a grapevine transplanted by God. He took the vine out of Egypt, cleared a fertile patch for it and built a protective wall around it. But then He broke down the wall of the vineyard and allowed a wild boar to ravage ('kircem', *to tear apart*) it and *Zīz śāday* to feed on it.

The overtones of *feed on it* are normally quite ambiguous. The Hebrew is 'raah', which means *graze like sheep* or *cattle* can also be rendered *be amongst friends* as well as simply *evil*. However, with the addition of 'kircem', *to tear apart,* in the mix, there's no doubt that here Ziz is meant to convey devastating ruin.

Yet, again, *Zīz śāday* is translated as *insects, things that move, wild animals, creatures of the field* and *beasts of the wilderness*—but still no mention of *birds*. Let alone one that resembles a gigantic, eclipse-producing, griffin-like monster.

Basically if we examine related words and concepts, 'ziz' comes down to a *large cluster of moving things*. Essentially, that's the concept behind the word. Hence hordes of insects,[5] herds of cattle, flocks of goats, mobs of sheep, bands of wild dogs, packs of wolves or any group of a similar nature which is capable of rapid shifts of movement could qualify as a 'ziz'. The word doesn't describe a solitary creature; it has an overtone of profusion to it. In fact, one of the meanings given for 'ziz' in its third appearance in Isaiah is *abundance*. Its overall resonance is *lots of living things that are moving back and forth*. So, it's fair to say that a wheeling flight of birds as in Psalm 50:11 could describe 'ziz'.

When it comes to eclipses, there's a strange phenomenon that just might account for its association with a monstrous fluttering Ziz. In the moments right before totality during a solar eclipse, mysterious undulating bands of shadow appear to hurtle across the landscape. It is not known what causes these thin wavy lines of alternating light and dark, but they can be seen rippling in parallel on plain-coloured surfaces immediately before and after a total solar eclipse.[6] Now bearing in mind that heaven and earth were considered by the people of Israel as witnesses who could be called upon to testify to the covenant between God and His people, just so light and shadow are regarded as living entities—not inanimate abstractions. Thus the racing movement of shadow bands during an eclipse could certainly qualify as a 'ziz'.

Yet by far the most significant word related to 'ziz' in my view has nothing to do with movement. This particular word is an incredibly momentous one through all of salvation history. It's 'mezuzah', *doorpost* or *gatepost*, and its central syllable is directly derived from 'ziz'.

Just as the name for the Python spirit is hidden within the Hebrew word for a *defiled threshold*, 'miphtan', so the name for the spirit of forgetting is hidden inside the word for *doorpost*.

There should be no surprise therefore that a mezuzah is about remembering God.

> *You shall therefore lay up these words of Mine in your heart and in your soul, and you shall bind them as a sign on your hand, and they shall be as frontlets between your eyes. You shall teach them to your children, talking of them when you are sitting in your house, and when you are walking by the way, and when you lie down, and when you rise. You shall* ***write them on the doorposts of your house and on your gates****, that your days and the days of your children may be multiplied in the land that the Lord swore to your fathers to give them, as long as the heavens are above the earth. For if you will be careful to do all this commandment that I command you to do, loving the Lord your God, walking in all His ways, and holding fast to Him, then the Lord will drive out all these nations before you, and you will dispossess nations greater and mightier than you.*

Every place on which the sole of your foot treads shall be yours.

Deuteronomy 11:18–24 ESV

Observant Jews, even today, wrap leather thongs around their arms and their brows to bind small boxes to themselves as the *sign* and the *frontlet* of God's command here in Deuteronomy. These small boxes—called 'tefillin' in modern Hebrew and 'phylacteries' in English—contain small scrolls of parchment or vellum with Scriptural verses written on them.

For thousands of years, the Jewish people have taken very literally God's directive to remember His saving acts and His goodness towards those who keep His covenant. The word 'tefillin' is not found in the Bible. Its meaning is unknown, though some scholars consider it to come from the Aramaic 't'phillim' which is the plural of 't'phillah', *prayer.*[7] Others consider that it derives from 'pelilah', meaning *evidence* or *justice.*[8]

On the other hand, the word 'phylactery' definitely *is* found in Scripture. Jesus uses it when He describes the self-aggrandisement of the scribes and Pharisees:

'Everything they do is done for people to see: They make their phylacteries wide and the tassels on their garments long...'

Matthew 23:5 NIV

'Phylactery' has different overtones of meaning to 'tefillin'. The dictionary defines it as coming from Greek 'phylakter' meaning *watcher* or *guard*. This in turn derives from 'phylaktḗrion', *outpost, safeguard, amulet,* based on a stem of 'phylássein', *to protect, guard.*[9]

This sense of *watching, safeguarding* and *protecting* is also found in the Jewish understanding of the modern mezuzah. Where once the mezuzah was understood to be the doorpost itself, now it more generally refers to the decorative case attached to the doorpost. These cases—whether plain wood, simple ceramic or fine metal, intricately worked and encrusted with jewels—contain specific verses from Deuteronomy, beginning with: '*Hear, O Israel! The Lord our God, the Lord is One.*' (Deuteronomy 6:4 NAS)

Henry Malone in his book, *Portals to Cleansing: taking back your land from the hands of the enemy*, suggests that the root of 'mezuzah' is 'zuz', meaning *turning around*, and that it refers to the movement of the door pivoting on the hinge. Certainly this would bring in the sense of 'ziz', *things that move back and forth*—however, it's worth noting that the original mezuzah was the immovable doorpost rather than the moving hinge. The modern mezuzah case with its inscribed scroll tucked tightly inside is placed near the hinge and then fastened to the doorpost with a dedication taken from Deuteronomy 20:5 and Psalm 30.

Malone tells of the ceremony of blessing and dedication described in Ruth Specter Lacelle's book, *Jewish Faith and the New Covenant*. To begin, a blessing is recited: 'Blessed art thou, O Lord, our God, King of the Universe who hast made us holy with Thy commandments and Who has commanded us to fasten the mezuzah.' A prayer follows: 'Master of the Universe, look down from

Thine holy habitation and accept in mercy and favour the prayer of Thy children who are here gathered to dedicate their dwelling and offer their thanksgiving. Grant them that they may live in their homes in brotherhood and friendship.'

Traditionally, these mezuzot (plural of 'mezuzah') which are placed near the hinge are decorated with the Hebrew letter 'shin': ש. This letter is said to stand for 'Shaddai'. This is of course one of the names of God—the one usually translated *almighty*. However, it's also considered to be an acronym. In Hebrew, 'shaddai' is just three letters: שדי (shin, dalet, yod). These three letters when applied to a mezuzah are considered to be shorthand for the phrase, '**Sh**omer **D**altot **Y**israel', *Guardian of Israel's Doors.*

So the 'shin' ש on a mezuzah is seen as symbolic of both 'shaddai', *almighty/nurturer*, and 'shomer', *guardian*. 'Shomer' ultimately comes from the word for *watchtower*. And it means that, as we apply this principle of guardianship to people, then we find that the job profile of a watchman has an unexpected aspect. Anyone who has the role of a guardian, a gatekeeper, a look-out, a monitor, a sentinel, a sentry, a doorkeeper, a janitor, a porter, a concierge, a caretaker, a custodian, a security officer—anyone who is in charge of keys, who is put on watch, who is called to discern the intentions of others coming and going—is also entrusted with protecting and nurturing memory.

This is true in the natural and in the spiritual.

A good memory is critical to the role of a watchman.[10] This is why so many people who are called to the spiritual office of watchman experience sustained, unremitting attacks against their minds. It's very true that trauma and ageing impact on memory but it's equally true that memory loss often has an overlooked spiritual component to be addressed in prayer.

Since the name Ziz is found within the Hebrew word, 'mezuzah'[11]—a word conceived of as describing a *guardian* of a doorway, as well as a *memorial* to God's saving acts and a *sign* of God's promise of *abundant* favour for honouring Him and keeping covenant—we can tell the office Ziz originally held before it was cast out of heaven. It was a sentinel angel charged with reminding humanity of God's wondrous deeds in times past.

Everything that God gives us as a blessing in life, the satan—our enemy and adversary—attempts to counterfeit so that curses will rain down on us instead. The satan's goal is to reverse and ruin the very things God gives us for our safety. So it is that Ziz, once an angelic majesty in charge of remembrance, is now a spiritual power constantly tempting us to forget.

Prayer

I strongly recommend that all the prayers in this book are read through carefully before being prayed aloud with intentionality. If you feel a check in your spirit from the Holy Spirit about any aspect of the prayer, then heed it. Put off the prayer until you receive permission from God.

It is vitally important to recognise that prayer is about relationship with the Father. It is not intended as a formula. The prayers in this book are meant to be guidelines to help you realign yourself with the holy Trinity; they are nothing in themselves; they are meant as a starting point, not an end in themselves.

Transformation is only possible as you hold onto the hem of Jesus' prayer shawl and ask Him to mediate before the Father for you. In the end, it's all about Him!

El Shaddai, Almighty Lord, strong-breasted one, I come by faith into Your presence. Thank You for reassuring, nurturing, comforting and parenting me. You have gifted me with so much. I confess that I have sinned in failing to acknowledge, appreciate or even notice many of these precious gifts. Among these is the treasure store of memory. I failed to even see my memory as a gift from You. I am sorry. I repent for my ingratitude and ask Your forgiveness for my lack of appreciation. Please forgive me. I have been blind. Please restore my sight.

Lord, as a parent I have failed to nurture and foster the full potential of memory in each of my children. You gave me the seed but it has been up to me to water and cherish it to life. I am sorry. Please forgive me for failing to be the parent You called me to be.

Forgive me also for the many times I have *wanted* to forget. The spirit of forgetting tempted me and I was seduced into thinking that it held out a better option to me than You did. I realise now that I agreed with the enemy rather than with Jesus. It seemed easier to forget than to remember, acknowledge, forgive and hand over the pain in Jesus' name. I am sorry I decided to believe these lies and today I choose to come out of agreement with the spirit of forgetting. Forgive me, El Shaddai, for each and every time I have succumbed to the temptation. Please forgive me for taking the bait of the enemy. Alert me to its ploys and schemes.

Lord, You know that deep in my spirit I have harboured the pain of offence. I ask You to take me by faith to the land of Gad, Reuben and Manasseh—the land of Gilead—and to pour the balm of that place into my wounded heart. Ease the ache and erase the unforgiveness; blot out my offences by the power of Jesus' blood.

Write there instead: 'El Elohim Yahweh! El Elohim Yahweh! He knows!'

He knows I choose forgiveness and ask Jesus to empower it; *He knows* I choose memory and ask Him to soothe the pain. I ask Him to set a memorial in my spirit this very day that I have chosen Him—El Shaddai and El Elohim Yahweh—as my Lord forevermore.

I acknowledge that, without You, I am helpless. I need Your help to retrain and re-*member* the dismembered neural pathways in my brain so I can remember to call on You. Forgetting is a ploy of the enemy. Memory is Your gift to me. I choose Your gifts and I ask You for the grace to make those gifts effective in my life.

I ask all this in the name of Jesus of Nazareth—the One who died that I could have life and have it to the fullest.

2

Remember, Remember

Sometime in the late seventies, my eldest brother was teaching his younger brother to drive. They would head out on back roads and one day by a lake they noticed a Pale Faced Rosella caught in a barbed wire fence. The unfortunate bird was pinned by its wing, and covered in ants as well as congealed blood.

They rescued him and brought him home. Then they cleaned him up and put him in a large cage with more than twenty adult budgerigars. My youngest brother was eleven at the time and planning to make his first million from breeding budgies.

Rosella fitted in well. He was incredibly cute. When he recovered from his injuries, he would lie on his back on the floor of the cage with his legs in the air, elegantly nibbling on the special grass seed my mum collected for the budgies. As well as being endearing and loveable, he was a show-off.

Not only that, he was a rosella with a big heart. When a mother budgie died suddenly, he took over the care and feeding of her five babies.

Budgerigars, both male and female, feed their young by eating seed and then regurgitating it for the chicks. Rosella, being so much bigger than the budgies, could effortlessly feed five babies in the time any other parent could feed one. His caring nature continued to come out. When another mother budgie died, he stepped into the breach and fed her young too. Then another mother died. Same thing—Rosella took over and fed the tiny clan.

My mum was starting to get suspicious. The dead budgies had all been healthy. There was no sign of illness or injury until they were mysteriously found on the floor of the cage. No other birds were dying. Only the mothers. And even though there was no mark on them, not even the slightest speck of blood, mum suspected Rosella. She and my youngest brother took turns to watch the cage.

One day, she saw Rosella do something strange. Without warning he pounced on another mother budgie and plucked out a tail feather. With that same daintiness he'd used to nibble on the grass seeds, he now held the quill to his beak and seemed to relish sucking on it, like a rare delicacy. Half a minute later, he pounced on the same bird and killed her.

Everyone loved Rosella but mum told my youngest brother he had to go. 'Good!' he said 'I can get forty bucks for him!' In the seventies, that was a *lot* of money.

But mum said he'd cost us nothing and he'd given us a lot of pleasure. Besides, what would God want us to do? 'Let him go free,' my brother replied. But Rosella had other ideas. Set free into the wild, he came and sat on top of the cage for weeks. Our neighbours often commented on the 'beautiful blue bird' that remained there, day after day.

Before long there were two 'beautiful blue birds' sitting on the cage. When Eastern Rosellas or Pale Faced Rosellas mate they do so for life. Not long afterwards, the pair flew away together. They returned a year later and together sat on the top of the budgie cage for another two or three weeks. This went on for several years. Mum liked to think they had a long and happy life together.

But reflecting on this story in the light of Ziz, she began to see it differently. Not from the perspective of a poor traumatised rosella who'd developed killer tendencies but from the perspective of the doomed mothers. When Rosella pounced on them, they were overshadowed by a giant that blotted out the sun. Rosella was the monstrous death-dealing eclipse—its actions in the natural were eerily similar to those of Ziz in the spiritual.

Budgies can die of fright and these mothers probably did. But what about Rosella's sucking on the quill? What was that about? There was a sense of something vampiric and ritualistic about it. It seems almost certain, in retrospect, that Rosella plucked out a blood feather—unlike a normal feather with a hollow shaft, a blood feather is one in the tail or wings with a blood supply.

And what about the babies? Suddenly my mum realised that Rosella would soon have undivided loyalty from the increasing number of budgies he nurtured. In a short time, his devoted 'family' would outnumber all the other birds in the cage—and Rosella would have ruled, unopposed.

Rosella never got the chance to test that undivided loyalty, but that doesn't mean to say the same is true of Ziz.

All of the threshold spirits—the fallen cherubim and seraphim—naturally desire undivided loyalty. They want us to confess that they, not Jesus of Nazareth, are lords of all. The word 'confess' simply means *come into agreement with*, which is why we can both confess our sins and confess that God is great. We are simply agreeing, in the first instance, that we have sinned and that we need God's remedy for it and, in the second instance, we're agreeing that God is worthy of praise and worship.

There are two levels of agreement with fallen spirits in my view. Complicity and covenant.

Many people cry out in anguish to God, 'But *I* have not covenanted with these angels!' And that is quite true. In the modern age, very few people have any true idea of what covenant is, so it's quite impossible for them to personally cut one with a fallen spirit. However complicity is another story. When we do nothing about a dark covenant coming down our family line, then we simply allow it to continue on its destructive path. We are in tacit, passive agreement with its existence: we are complicit.

God is constantly telling us, in manifold ways, about the existence of these ungodly covenants. He uses dreams and nightmares, the patterns of our lives and our recurring problems, the language we use to describe our feelings about events. He even uses enigmatic and faintly disturbing images like a rosella sucking on a blood feather before killing a smaller bird.

Many people have contacted me about their nightmares featuring snakes they recognise as being pythons. Often in the dreams, the python is sitting on a doorstep, barring their way in or out of their house. Now it doesn't take any skill at all in dream interpretation to know that this is a warning about the spirit of Python—which, like Ziz, is a threshold spirit. God is simply saying: 'Be alert! Be on your guard! Pray without ceasing! Python has a right to test your choices as you make decisions about your calling. Pray to make the right *choice* for the right *reason*.'

I believe that Python belongs to the class of angels called the cherubim. I think there is sufficient evidence in Scripture to say that's fairly certain.[12] The cherubim are actually stationed on the threshold itself.

However there are other spirits who, while not positioned exactly on the threshold, are nevertheless in the immediate vicinity. Such spirits include Leviathan and Ziz. Because they are allies, I believe they are probably of the same order and therefore, because Leviathan seems to be a seraph, I conclude Ziz is the same.

Now it's also my belief that these threshold spirits belong to the group called 'exousia', *powers*. In Ephesians 6:12, speaks of 'arche', *principalities*, 'exousia', *powers*, and 'kosmokrators', *world rulers*. My understanding is that Paul is describing a hierarchy—the 'exousia' are higher in rank than the principalities and lower in rank than the world-rulers. As I see it, principalities—angelic princes—have authority over geographical areas such as cities or nations and world rulers have, as their name implies, authority over worlds. It is when it comes to *powers* that my views differ from that of many other people: the 'exousia', in my opinion, have authority over thresholds—that is, over *transitional* places, times and states of change. They are not limited to the geographical sphere, they also claim authority over certain times and states of being.

In the natural, we might understand transitional imagery in terms of doorways, gateways, boundaries, frontiers, bridges, shorelines, New Year periods, dawn, sunset, birth, death, ocean bars, the sound barrier, melting of ice, the evaporation of water into steam. All these things in the natural have liminal aspects—thresholds describe an in-between place, moment or state. And, as in the natural, so in the spiritual: thresholds in our world have an equivalent in heavenly places.

When we are complicit with the guardians of these spiritual thresholds regarding covenantal agreements with them, we are effectively retaining a pledge to serve the enemies of God. Now God, in His extraordinary mercy, may still stand in harm's way for a time because of our ignorance. But eventually our ignorance becomes wilful in the face of His repeated attempts to inform us about the truth of our situation.

Sometimes the only way God can get through to us about the horrendous consequences of our ungodly covenants is to let us experience a small taste of those consequences. Of course, to us, it feels like a huge, bitter, poisoned chalice He's forcing us to drink.

We mistake His mercy for misery.

> *'...you meant evil against me, but God meant it for good in order to bring about this present result, to preserve many people...'*
>
> Genesis 50:20 NAS

Joseph was the favoured son of Jacob who gave him a coat-of-many-colours. His story opens with the comment that, at seventeen years of age, he made the lives of his brothers miserable by telling tales on them. They returned the favour and made his life miserable by selling him as a slave. His cousins,[13] the Midianites,[14] were taking a caravan of myrrh and spices down to Egypt. They bought him and on-sold him in Egypt.

Joseph experienced thirteen years of misery before being catapulted in a single day from prison to prime minister. But eventually he was able to say to his brothers: '*...you meant evil against me, but God meant it for good...*' He recognised God's mercy.

His story is one of repeatedly forgetting and shredding the truth. Although Ziz is not mentioned in it, these themes repeat themselves in the events of Joseph's life. In fact, they're so strong, Joseph actually names his firstborn son, Manasseh, *forget*.

Hints of Leviathan occur when retaliation and backlash become evident early in the story. Perhaps this is intentionally foreshadowed by mentioning Dothan, the place where Joseph looks for his brothers. Dothan contains the element 'than', meaning *sea monster*, the same as the last syllable of Levia*than*.

Forgetting is evident in the action of Joseph's brothers who disregard their responsibility as brothers. It's also evident in the action of Joseph's cousins who likewise ignore family obligations. It's evident in the tearing of Joseph's coat, and the shredding of the truth as the brothers present the bloodied remnants to their father. Another coat quickly features when Joseph's cloak is torn from him by Potiphar's wife and she too uses it as evidence in the tearing apart of truth.

The cupbearer who promises to remember Joseph while he's in prison in fact forgets him. But 'reminded of his shortcomings' by Pharaoh's dreams, he recommends Joseph as a dream interpreter. This is the turning point: Joseph is released and Pharaoh is impressed with his skill and wisdom. Joseph, on coming to power, is given a new name.

> *'Pharaoh gave Joseph the name Zaphenath-Paneah and gave him Asenath daughter of Potiphera, priest of On, to be his wife.'*
>
> Genesis 41:45 NIV

Now logically this name-giving is actually a name covenant—an exchange. Any Pharaoh worth his salt who appointed someone straight out of jail without putting in some safeguards—like covenant obligations—would be a foolish ruler indeed.

As Rosella the budgie-killer showed, successful empire-building requires undivided loyalty—which is most efficiently accomplished by the feeding of the starving masses. But that only comes in later in Joseph's story. Still as everyone in ancient times knew, undivided loyalty was proclaimed through covenant.

And in fact, Scripture suggests that such a covenant did indeed exist between Joseph and the ruling House when it reports another Pharaoh arose who '*knew not Joseph*'. (Exodus 1:8 KJV) The word 'yada'', *know*, is sometimes used to indicate the individuals concerned had covenanted together.

The only hint of this in Scripture is the new name given to Joseph. If it is indeed a name covenant, then an exchange was involved. Such exchanges often playfully punned on the original bearer's name. If this is such a covenant, then the name of the Pharaoh (or a significant part of it) should be hidden within Zaphenath-Paneah. The 'zaph' of Zaphenath and the 'seph' of Joseph are almost rhyming, so that part probably goes back to Joseph's name.[15]

But the name of Joseph's wife, Asenath,[16] shares a common rhyming part with Zaphenath, so perhaps this is a clue as to the name of the Pharaoh. It would seem he should be 'enath' or something very similar, given that ancient Hebrew had no vowels.

In the king lists of Egypt, there appears to be only two Pharaohs whose names contain a syllable like 'enath'. One was Anat-her and the other, Aperanat,[17] who is arguably his son. They are considered to be Hyksos kings—Canaanite invaders.[18] Joseph had come from Canaan, so they would hardly have had a second thought about making a covenant with him.

Such a covenant would create obligations of mutual protection between the House of Pharaoh and the wider family of Joseph for as many generations as that dynasty ruled. But when the ruling line changed as the Hyksos were expelled from Egypt, any covenants made by previous Pharaohs would be nullified.

Now I think we can actually identify the Pharaoh of this story as Aperanat. The reason involves the names of Joseph's sons: Manasseh and Ephraim. I believe that parents name their children for the unresolved issues of their family line. And if Joseph did that then these names point to two things: first, *forgetting* and, second, *the death of Rachel.*

Joseph's mother died at Bethlehem Ephrathah, giving birth to his younger brother Benjamin. Now Ephraim and Ephrathah are closely linked names. However, Hebrew 'ephra-' is basically the same as Egyptian 'apera-', the start of Aperanat's name. Ephraim's name is a truly brilliant fusion, commemorating both Joseph's mother as well as the ruler he had covenanted with.

This turn in the storyline heralds a strong change from forgetting to remembering.

As his brothers bow before him, Joseph remembers his dreams.

As he accuses them of spying, they remember their treatment of him and conclude they are reaping what they sowed.

Reuben recalls how he told them not to sin and they didn't listen.

After a bit of deception and truth-tearing on Joseph's part, the happy-ever-after that began with his promotion to power rises to a whole new level. Joseph is lavish in forgiveness, unstinting in reconciliation, eager to see his father once more.

God reminds Jacob of His faithfulness and assures him He will be with him even in Egypt.

And at the end of Jacob's life, he remembers to do something for his sons that was never done for him: he spoke directly and prophetically into their callings. When Isaac had blessed Jacob, giving him the birthright meant for Esau, it was a generic pronouncement. It did nothing to awaken his unique and individual destiny—that calling hidden within each of our names.

It is this true destiny, this high calling of God, that Ziz wants to rip apart.

'Many colours' has the sense in Scripture of *grace*. When Joseph's coat-of-many-colours was torn, so was grace and truth through his entire family.

Through forgiveness, we are called to ease the famine of the heart in those around us and summon them into grace and truth.

When it comes to forgetting there are psychological and emotional components to consider, not just spiritual ones. Not everything is a spiritual problem. However, it's all too easy for Ziz to take advantage of a situation and turn it to a massive spiritual problem that spans more than one generation.

Forgetting is a natural part of crossing a threshold. You know that frustrating feeling when you go into another room to get something and then you stand there, blank, because you've forgotten what you came for? Researcher Gabriel Radvansky says that exiting or entering through a doorway can be a signal to the mind to file away a previous episode of activity and get ready for the new. The crossing of the doorway serves as an 'event boundary'.[19] His recommendations for overcoming the problem are: to mentally repeat the reason as you enter the room or else to announce aloud what you're about to do.

Such recommendations are similar to the very things God commanded the Israelites regarding their doorposts: to write and speak of His goodness of God there.

> *'Tie them as symbols on your hands and bind them on your foreheads. Write them on the doorframes of your houses and on your gates.'*
>
> Deuteronomy 6:8 NIV

And then He commanded them to go further: to constantly teach their children to love Him with all their hearts and minds and strength. To repeat the lesson over and over. This direction of God is there not just because we so easily forget, but because Ziz is only too willing to help us.

Western society has turned against rote learning—decades ago. Back when I was teaching mathematics, I was seen as quite a bit retrogressive. That's because my lessons were boring. Some of them incredibly and deliberately so. In one instance I realised that a particular high school mathematics class wasn't nearly as dim as they were painted. This group of Year 10 students simply didn't have good memories. They had no trouble with the process of finding the volume or the surface area of any solid object, *providing they were given the initial equation*. But if they didn't have the formula, they had no hope.

Now, I knew that, in the end-of-semester test, they would not be given any help. They simply had to know by heart over a dozen equations of varying difficulty. So every day I started the lesson with ten questions like: 'What is the volume of a cylinder? What is the surface area of a hemisphere?' Get all the answers right and the students could spend their time on their own projects. Get any wrong and they'd have to write out the correct formula ten times on the first day, twenty times on the second, forty times on the third, eighty times on the fourth... and so on, doubling all the time. The incentive truly was there to commit the equations to memory. And not surprisingly, my class blitzed the end-of-semester test.

A year later, I was filling in one day as a substitute for a Year 11 teacher who was absent. The lesson happened to be on the volumes and surface areas of solids. Looking around, I realised there were several students who'd been in my class the previous year. 'Right!' I picked one girl at random. 'You'll remember this. Tell me the surface area of a cone.'

'Miss, it's impossible to remember that after all this time!' She threw up her hands. And then she rattled off the formula, word-perfect.

'Excellent.' I wrote her answer on the board, and went on with the lesson.

She approached me at the end of class. 'Miss, how on earth did I know that answer?'

'Well, you wrote it out so many times last year, it's memorised forever. You'll be eighty, maybe with Alzheimer's, but you'll still know the surface area of a cone. Not that it's likely to be any use then. But, listen. You probably don't realise this formula is the hardest one you'll come across in the course you're now doing. So I'd say you can sail through this semester. You've already know what you need.'

Her eyes lit up, glowing with sudden hope. 'Miss, can you do this kind of thing for any subject?'

'Of course you can.'

Her face was transformed as she headed to the door. 'Thanks, Miss.' She greeted her waiting friends with a high-five. 'Wanna know how to pass any subject? I got the secret.'

Don't despise rote learning. The vast majority of people need repetition to forge neural pathways in their brains.

We need to deliberately and consciously choose the techniques God has given us.

As well as rote learning, there are other helpful things we can do to enhance our memories. We can repeat to ourselves His command as often as possible: to remember that He is one and we are called to love Him with all our heart, mind, soul and strength. We could also put 'memory verses' in this category of learning things off by heart.

We should teach our children memory is valuable, and that old-fashioned games like the 'memory tray' full of random objects are worthwhile playing regularly.

Repetitive actions and words are helpful, as well as simply writing things down. Speaking them aloud as you write is even more helpful. And memory enhancement is, of course, assisted by exercise, sleep, relaxation, laughter and diet. There are foods—and oils—that help us retain memory.

Mysteriously, however, those essential oils are connected to particular names—names we'll look at in a later chapter.

Prayer

Father, El Shaddai, El Elohim Yahweh, help me learn the lessons hidden in the story of Rosella:

> Well-intentioned actions (*putting Rosella in a safe place away from predators*) can have devastating results for others (*death of mother budgerigars*).

Abba Father, I acknowledge and repent of the times I have failed to be watchful and alert to the dangers resulting from my actions. Open my eyes, Father, and forgive me for the times my good intentions destroyed others.

> Seemingly altruistic actions (*Rosella feeding the orphan budgies*) can hide a hidden agenda of empire-building by bonding with the motherless babies and securing their undivided loyalty.

Lord, keep me from judging the motives of others but never allow me to be blind to the evidence of ungodly actions. Keep me alert to unholy possibilities and mindful that things are not always what they seem to be. Forgive me for wanting to overlook the obvious. Forgive me too for the times when the truth has been revealed, the offender exposed and I chose the easy way of non-confrontation. The offender was endearing and charming and I allowed myself to be seduced, even though my heart warned me that all was not as it seemed. Father, I recognise that I closed my eyes to both the truth and to Your warnings. Where chaos has reigned as a result of my actions, forgive me and teach me to listen to Your voice and that Your way is the only way.

> When Rosella was evicted, he seemed so beautiful as he hung around, trying to get back in. But he was just awaiting an opportunity to rebuild his empire.

Teach me, Father, that sin may seem beautiful, even when I've kicked it out of my life. I acknowledge that forgetting is still an appealing temptation. However, to allow it re-entry into my life is to knowingly invite havoc. Thank You, Abba, that Jesus' blood can cancel even this deliberately deeper level of sin. Forgive me, Father, for even thinking of allowing bad habits back into my life.

> When all else failed, Rosella left and went far away—but not before he made several more attempts at lengthy intervals to regain entry into the safe haven. He never forgot the kingdom he was building and lost.

Forgive me, Father, for underestimating the power of sin. I have underestimated its power to tempt and entice. Father, thank You for the life lessons learned from Rosella. He was cute. He was beautiful. He was resourceful. He appeared so self-less but in reality everything he did was totally self-serving. Forgive me, Father, for the times I have acted just like Rosella.

In Jesus' name. Amen.

3

Bridge of Birds

I first became aware of the spirit of forgetting—though not as Ziz—way back when I was researching the symbology of my childhood nightmares. Every so often I would come across a remarkable insight into my fears as a child and sometimes, with enthusiasm and excitement, I would share these fresh revelations with family members. On more than one occasion, I was taken aback by my sister-in-law's comment: 'You told me this three months ago.'

And I'd think: 'That's impossible! I didn't know this until yesterday—and it's not the sort of thing I'd ever forget.'

So I began to write things down. And, to my fearful dismay, I started to find scraps of paper in my own handwriting with significant information on them that I had no memory of ever recording. The more of them I found the more I was convinced I was losing my mind as well as my memory.

The turning point was one terrible week when I forgot I was supposed to lead a meeting; I forgot an important appointment; I forgot a major deadline; I forgot the safe place I'd put a whole bundle of test papers to mark; I forgot I'd said I'd fill in for someone on playground duty; I forgot where I put my glasses and spent half an hour looking for them, only to discover them perched on my head; I forgot my keys as I left the house and accidentally locked myself out. That was the moment I collapsed and went to God. He seemed to have been waiting for me. 'Am I losing my mind,' I asked, 'or are You trying to tell me something?'

His mind-voice radiated calm. 'When did this series of disasters start?'

I hadn't expected a question. 'Well, come to think of it, it would be last Sunday.'

'And what were you doing immediately before this started?'

I racked my brains. All I could think of was a discussion after the church service on the problems that Christianity would face in the next twenty years. My contribution to the conversation had been that I thought one of the biggest issues believers would face in the future would be that they would forget they had dabbled ever so briefly in witchcraft, buying one or two magazines on the occult before discarding the practice—and that, having forgotten, they would have no idea why their lives were such a mess.

'Think about what the minister said in reply,' said the Lord.

'Oh, yes.' It came back to me in a rush. He'd talked about the time he'd pastored a church in an area renowned for its witchcraft covens. Suddenly it clicked. I spent more than ten years, going to that very same area each summer as part of a beach mission team that presented a Christian holiday programme for children. 'Was I a target?' I asked the Lord.

'Of course,' He said. 'You were a leader so you were an especial target. And the frustration you've been experiencing this last week has been a sustained attempt to distract you from remembering that conversation. It's come very close to success. The spirit of forgetting has been working overtime on your case.'

'There is a *spirit* of forgetting?' Light-bulb moment. That explained so much. I thought of all the scraps of paper I could never remember writing. A *spirit* of forgetting? Aha!

'Its current agenda is to stop you from praying about the curses spoken over you as a beach mission leader.'

'So what do I do about it?'

'It has rights you cannot even begin to imagine. So don't even think about binding it—that will only make things worse. Don't think about casting it out—it will try to tear you apart. What I suggest you do is ask Me to remind you that you've forgotten something whenever it attacks you. And then to ask Me to give back to you, as you go searching for what you've lost, *more* than the spirit of forgetting ever took from you.'

I didn't understand why this spirit should have such rights—not for many years. But the Lord's strategy sounded good to me. It was clearly a variation on *'all things work together for good for those who love God and are called according to His purpose.'* If allowing the spirit of forgetting to continue in my life could, in God's redemptive purpose, ultimately lead to still-greater remembrance, then I was up for it. Even if the spirit of forgetting did its worst, that would only mean that God would show Himself even stronger on my behalf.

'Bring it on!' I thought. 'I'm ready.'

Ready? *Ha!* How naïve! The reality was that I only had the tiniest pieces of a jigsaw puzzle. However God was busy throwing more into my lap.

A colleague at work lost her keys. Maree—her name, though I didn't know it at the time, was very significant—had driven home and then been unable to find the keys to enter her house. This was decidedly odd, since the car keys and the house keys were on the same ring. Despite many thorough searches of her own as well as those of family members, the keys remained elusive. But they had to be around and close by: it was impossible for her to have driven home in the first place without those keys.

Yet a whole day went by without their reappearance, another, a third. Maree, her husband and her children had turned the house upside down by this stage as they searched for them. Because the keys were so old and unique, the doors were effectively locked shut and the only access to the house was via a second-storey window.

Maree had her workmates in stitches during the lunch hour as she laughed in recollection of how the guests to a dinner party she'd arranged had had to climb up a ladder into the second-floor window. The 'case of the vanishing keys' was becoming more memorable with each passing day.

A week later the keys still hadn't turned up. And Maree was absent from work. Then she was absent a second day. That was rare enough to cause comment in our staffroom.

I rang her to ask if she was ill. 'I'm being torn apart,' she said. 'I know I laughed about the visitors having to climb through the window but it was terrible. I am so mortified I can't face anyone. I need space to put myself back together.'

I resonated with the words 'torn apart'. They drove my mind back to the terrible week when I'd been assailed by the spirit of forgetting. 'I'm coming over,' I said.

Maree lived just a five minute's drive from work. On the way, I asked God for a solution—and what came to mind was so strange I wasn't sure how to present it to her. 'I'm sure you've tried everything,' I said after we'd exchanged a few pleasantries. 'So you might just be desperate enough to try something a bit different. It will probably sound weird and, if it doesn't work, you can put it down to Annie's eccentricity. It's not going to hurt—it will probably just feel foolish.'

Maree was indeed desperate enough to try almost anything.

So I said, 'I think you should take off the necklace you're wearing.'

Her mouth dropped open. 'You know,' she said, 'just before you said that, I knew that was exactly what you were going to say.'

Maree's necklace was an exquisite silver design of Celtic knotwork. She'd been wearing it for several weeks. It came from grateful Irish relatives who'd enjoyed her generous hospitality for a three-month holiday in Australia. It was delicate, lovely and of the highest workmanship. The design celebrated one of the legendary tragedies of Celtic mythology: the tale of the Children of Llyr.

'Talk me through this,' she said. 'I'm not resisting. I just want to understand.'

'Recently,' I told her, 'I discovered the existence of a spirit of forgetting. This issue started with forgetting. You put the keys down and have forgotten where. However, keys are also about authority at doorways. So I'm postulating the existence of the spirit who claims some sort of authority in your household. I don't really know what I'm talking about but I figure, if there is such a spirit, it's probably to do with keys and doorways and thus I'm going to pick on Janus, the Roman god of the doorway. Words like "January" and "janitor" are related to his.'

Maree nodded and touched the necklace gingerly. 'But it's not January and this is not symbolic of Janus.'

'True. It's symbolic of Llyr—but, according to some mythographers, the Celtic equivalent of Janus is Llyr.[20] Moreover, I would like to point out that this is the first week of November which may not be the first week of the ordinary year but is the first week of the Celtic year.'

Maree figured she had nothing to lose. What I was suggesting was so simple that it was worth trying. I prayed and she took off the necklace.

I got back to work about ten minutes later and a phone message was waiting for me: '*I found them!*'

It turned out that Maree's keys had been in a place she'd searched nearly a dozen times, her husband had searched just as many and her children had also repeatedly searched. She estimated various people had looked thirty times in the exact spot where they were finally discovered. No one had seen them. Or, if they had, they immediately forgot that they did.

It seemed incredible that such a simple action as removing a necklace should make such a difference. And, no doubt, many people would consider the whole episode nothing more than coincidence. But I had long ago reached the point where I no longer had any time for the concept of 'coincidence'.

God was making a point.

I can look back now and see the fingerprints of the spirit of forgetting all over the situation: from the threshold objects—keys—to the threshold time—the first week of the Celtic year. In addition, the reaction of laughter and the feeling of being torn apart are critical indicators of the spiritual background to the issue.

Mark Wolynn describes the importance of language in exposing the roots of generational trauma.[21] He relates the story of a nineteen year old student who woke up one night, shivering, racked by the obsessive thought that if he fell back to sleep he'd die. Night after night, the student stayed up, tormented by a sense that his life depended on staying awake. His grades fell and he was unable to continue his studies. As Wolynn explored the language of the problem, he came to focus on 'freezing' and 'awake'—and so uncovered the family trauma that had passed down to this boy. His uncle had been a linesman who had gone out to fix an electrical fault when a snowstorm suddenly blew up. His body was found the next day. He was just nineteen years old when he died of hypothermia—the same age as the student who, out-of-time, experienced the feelings and stresses of his uncle's last hours.

Repeatedly, Wolynn uses his client's language descriptors as the key to unlock the trauma of the past. In some cases, such as this one, there is no direct genetic link between the person suffering in one generation and in a previous one. Many of us would like to believe the past is a forgotten country we can leave behind us, but unresolved trauma affects our descendants in clinically specific ways.

It affects us too.

Just as Wolynn found language was the key to recognising generational trauma, so too it can be used to identify the spiritual source of current stresses. When we use words like *strangled, throttled, choked, squeezed, crushed, squashed* and so on, we are in fact sensing the presence of the threshold guardian Python—the spirit of constriction.

On the other hand, when we use words like *retaliation, whiplash, kickback, backfire* or *fallout*, we're sensing an entirely different entity: Leviathan—the spirit of backlash.

We need to pay attention to our words and to the feelings that accompany them. Feelings are so often valuable clues to the precise nature of the spiritual problem. When we use words like *spread too thin, overextended, burning the candle at both ends* or alternatively *withering* or *squandered*, we're sensing Rachab—the spirit of wasting.

So what words describe Ziz, the spirit of forgetting? Ones like: *torn apart, shredded, gutted, ripped up, going crazy, nuts, mad.*

By the time Maree had searched for her keys a half dozen times, she feared she was going mad. How was it possible to drive home and lose the keys in the few steps between the car and the house?

The Celtic seagod Llyr has, with a little help from William Shakespeare, become associated with insanity. Llyr Half-Speech first moved into the shadowy space of half-legend-half-history as Leir of Leicester. According to a medieval chronicle, Leir lived around the time of the prophet Elijah and was the longest-reigning king of the ancient Britons.[22] Shakespeare's play, *King Lear*, takes the basic story of this legendary ruler and reworks it to depict a gradual descent into insanity. Unlike the original tale with its happy ending, *King Lear* is a tragedy.

Forgetfulness, madness, a mind in chaos and confusion: sometimes these things have spiritual aspects to them.[23]

My sister and I got talking about childhood nightmares. To our amazement, we discovered that we both remembered haunting dreams which shared the same bizarre symbolism: witches that were disguised as clothing. Where had an idea like that come from?

'Did you ever have a dream about a wave?' my sister asked me.

'No.'

'I haven't ever been able to understand mine. I've always loved the sea but this dream was unbelievably horrible.' My sister went on to describe the nightmare in some detail. It was about a wave as high as heaven. Slow-moving, inexorable, it was the mother of all tsunamis, the stormsurge to end all stormsurges.

As my sister continued her description, I suddenly found myself arguing with her. 'No, that's not how it goes,' I insisted. 'Back up.' And I'd launched into a description of an entirely different ending. I was baffled: *how had I not remembered the dream until my sister started to get it wrong?* Not that, of course, she really got it wrong. Just different.

As I started to 'correct' her account, she exclaimed: 'You've made me remember other dreams I'd entirely forgotten. There were different versions!'

In a rash moment, I promised my sister I'd find out what the dream meant. I was fortunate in my research that I never realised this nightmare is not particularly unusual. JRR Tolkien suffered from it, so did his son Christopher, so did the artist Albrecht Dürer, so did my sister's daughter and several of my colleagues and friends.

Tolkien believed his to be a racial memory of a long-ago event.

Mark Wolynn talks about family trauma travelling down bloodlines three or four generations. But what about world trauma so deep, so harrowing, that all anyone wants to do is forget it?

In its final form my wave nightmare contained a startling tidbit of information I have never been able to confirm with solid evidence. I have no objective proof verifying my consequent belief that Alzheimer's Disease[24] has a huge spiritual component, except this dream. So take it whatever way you will.

I can date the dream to the mid-sixties—a time period long before 'Alzheimers' became a common word in our modern cultural vocabulary.

In its most elaborate, final form, the nightmare went like this:

> I went out to the clothes-line behind our house and noticed four car mats flapping in the breeze. I realised that the witches—who in previous dreams had disguised themselves as midnight blue dresses—had now transformed themselves into rubber mats for the floor of a car. As I approached them, I sensed the witches were dormant; their power reduced to effectively nothing. But abruptly one of them woke, red eyes blazing. She shrieked an alert and flew at me.
>
> I ran. The witch's power might be vastly diminished but it was still enough to kill. By the time I hurtled into the family car, my sister and brothers had appeared out of nowhere to join me. We got the car moving; I took charge of the steering wheel, one brother

worked the gear stick and another operated the brake and accelerator. My sister sat in the passenger seat cradling my baby brother. Off we sped down the road.

By the time we reached the town hall in the next suburb, we'd lost the witches. But we felt we needed expert advice to get rid of them for good. So we decided we'd visit my grandfather who had just moved into an aged care village. He wasn't home when we arrived but a neighbour told us where he'd gone. We decided we'd try to catch up with him.

As we were about to leave, I noticed some wildflowers wrapped in tissue paper on my grandfather's doorstep. I knew they'd been left for me. No, I felt they'd always *belonged* to me. I hesitated about taking them, however. They'd get crushed if I tried to hold them while steering the car. Reluctantly—for their own safety—I left the wildflowers behind.

We drove off and our car soon reached a bridge renowned as the longest in the world. It crossed the mouth of a river as it emptied into the sheltered bay.[25]

To our surprise, there was no toll collector at the toll gate so we simply drove round the barrier and on to the bridge. But halfway across, the car stalled. Nothing we tried would get it started again. As we were considering our options—to go forward or back—we noticed a huge wave rolling in from the open ocean. It was monstrous—reaching far into the heavens. But fortunately it was moving with snail-like slowness. I decided to run back to the toll booth at the start of the bridge, find the toll collector and convince him to help us.

The toll collector looked strange. He wasn't wearing the usual uniform—instead he had on a sheepskin vest and around his neck was a tiny horn on a thong. His face was in shadow—invisible. He tried to convince me to go into one of the towers at the end of the bridge. There, he assured me, I'd be safe from the gargantuan wave. In the meantime, he'd go after my siblings. I felt very dubious about his reassurances. I had no reason to be suspicious but I felt he was entirely wrong about the tower as a safe refuge.

I was about to give in to his persuasions when he saw several cars in the distance and left to put up a barrier to block access to the bridge. I took the opportunity to slip away around the side of the bridge. There I noticed that the pylons under the towers were not concrete, as I expected—they were constructed of massive rainbows that arched down from the sky and merged with the pylons.

In trying to find a way back onto the bridge, I found myself splashing across a mudbank towards some small fishing booths. I opened one door, hoping to find help. As I stepped inside, I was overwhelmed by the sensation that this was a perfect sanctuary from the wave. I could stay here and be safe.

There was a knock at the door. The toll collector had come after me. He urged me to leave the booth and return to the tower. But I was reluctant to go. I knew I would lose the sense of safety the moment I stepped out the door.

In addition, there was something increasingly peculiar about the man. I could see him but I couldn't remember him. I kept staring at him, thinking, 'Why can't I remember what you look like?' I was conscious I could see his face but, by the time the image of his appearance had passed from my retina along my optic nerve to my brain, it had dissipated. In the nanosecond or so between eye and brain, the memory had completely faded. I could see the sheepskin coat and the tiny horn quite clearly and remember them—but his face was elusive.

He sensed my doubt and misgivings. 'Trust me,' he said finally. 'I'm an old friend of your family.'

I gave in and followed him back to the bridge, past the rainbow pylons and up to the toll booth. Just as we arrived, so did a group of cars. The drivers were agitated at the closure of the bridge and began arguing with the toll collector. He pointed to the huge oncoming wave but the drivers were undeterred by the danger. As the argument raged, I slipped away again. I couldn't take the chance on any of the fishing booths—they were the first place the toll collector would search. So, realising I could not reach my brothers and sisters in time, and hoping they had decided to walk to the other side of the bridge, I ran back along the riverbank, heading upstream.

In the distance, I heard a horn blowing, deep and mournful. I realised the toll collector had blown his tiny horn, warning of the end of the world. The wave was rushing up behind me. I sensed the tower had fallen. I ran on desperately, until I came to a green hill with a white church on it. Unable to go further, I turned to face the wave. It hurtled towards me and then, its last force spent, stopped just centimetres from my feet.

Mark Wolynn has worked a great deal with the descendants of Holocaust victims. In his counselling, he discovered that the unresolved trauma of previous generations, the hidden stories of terror, the horror that remains unspoken, does not go away simply because it is swept under a mental carpet. In some families the elephant-sized lump protruding from the shaggy pile may never be acknowledged—but dreams, emotions, and our verbal expression of feeling and fears sometimes shape our lives by their existence.

Wolynn posits that the temporary epigenetic superstructure on the DNA of traumatised people is meant to serve a very good function. Significant information is passed down to the next generation to help the family line survive similar traumatic events—and even, more importantly, to help avoid them in the future.

Some of this significant information is, I believe, spiritual in nature. This is often the most difficult kind to interpret because we've forgotten so many Scriptural principles—in some cases, getting them entirely back to front. When, for example, I first read Henry Clay Trumbull's explanation of how we'd reversed the original concept of the Passover because we didn't know how a threshold covenant worked, I was stunned. How could it possibly be, I wondered, that the blood of the lamb on the lintels and doorposts was not about keeping the Angel of Death *out* but about inviting God *in* as covenant defender? However, as I went back to the Bible, I saw that even the English wording did not contradict Trumbull's interpretation.

By that stage, I realised that the spirits of the threshold, Python in particular, will make use of any ambiguity in an attempt to deceive us.

Another way unspoken trauma of the past emerges in the present is through nightmares. Frequently these are dismissed as 'just a bad dream'. So, they are sent down a generation, unresolved. Even if they are not ignored, they are often too difficult to interpret—mostly, I've found, because the dream-images are the mind's best attempt to translate another language. What does a bridge with pylons made of rainbows mean?

Images in fiction are dismissed even more often than dreams as just vivid imagination. I used to succumb to the thought there was a rational explanation for the repeated imagery across fantasy novels. But now I think that, like repeated dreams, 'fictional' symbols are God's way of talking to us about the unresolved issues of our family lines. Memory of trauma will emerge, whether we like it or not, even if it's on the fringes.

Because this is the way God brings the sins of the fathers to our attention so we take action concerning them.

Sometimes people ask me to interpret their dreams. When they do, I want as much tiny detail as possible. What seems trivial or bizarre to the conscious mind is usually nothing of the kind. I can look back on my nightmare about the towering wave and realise it is a translation of concepts my twelve-year-old mind had no words for. There was no point in God giving me a verbal message I couldn't decipher; He gave me images which better explained my spiritual peril. If I'd been able to recognise and spell Old Icelandic, we could have had a conversation. But I was ignorant.[26]

And perhaps His additional reason for images rather than words is because He knew long it would take for me to comprehend His message. Pictures stick in the memory far longer than words.

My sister's dream took a different direction. But, between the symbolism of the two of them, I had plenty of fodder for research.

Fortunately I didn't encounter the story of Tolkien's nightmare until after I'd solved the riddle of their meaning or I would have gone in the wrong direction. As it was, every time I fell for some glib explanation by a psychologist or psychiatrist or dream counsellor, my sister would glare and pull me back into line. At last, I thought I had examined every possibility for what the dream meant—except one. The gigantic wave was symbolic of... a gigantic wave. As for the other elements of the dream, perhaps they too were symbolic of themselves.

Now these were the days before Google. Search engines were different back then. So once I considered the possibility the symbols were representative of themselves, things started to fall into place. A single name kept popping up repeatedly in my searches: the same symbols appeared in the poetry of Clive Hamilton. By the third time it happened, I was curious. Who was Clive Hamilton? Was it significant he had my surname?

Clive Hamilton turned out to be a pseudonym of CS Lewis. Getting hold of *Narrative Poems*, I read *Dymer* with a growing sense of unease. I recognised all his archetypal figures—they had appeared in dreams and writings for years. Significantly, where Lewis gave a name, I had an identical one.

By the time the guardian appeared at the end of the poem, I was horrified. *Hama*, I thought, as an angel! What were you thinking, Jack? I was even more horrified when I realised Lewis hadn't named the guardian. But I was so sure I was right in my identification of this character, I looked up the name. I found two equally likely possibilities for Hama—one in Old Norse, another in Latin.

My first discovery, however, was that Háma is a minor character in *The Lord of the Rings*—a door warden in the kingdom of Rohan and captain of the king's guard. Tolkien was perhaps inspired to choose his name from the earliest of English epics, *Beowulf*. This Anglo-Saxon name, is thought to refer to the Norse god Heimdall.

Months after I promised my sister I'd find out what the dream meant, I was finally closing in on the answer. In Norse mythology, Heimdall is the guardian of the rainbow bridge, Bifröst. He wore a sheepskin and, just prior to the battle at the end of the age, he sounded a horn to warn the gods of Asgard that a monstrous wave was approaching.

The toll collector on the bridge in my dream!

Tick, sheepskin garment.

Tick, horn.

Tick, bridge pylons as rainbows.

Tick, on guard.

Tick, end of the world.

Tick, monstrous wave.

As I explored the information and speculation about Heimdall across various authors, I found more and more of the detail of the dream.

Tick, tower.

Tick, booths.

Tick, witches embodied as clothing.

Some scholars questioned the identification of *Beowulf*'s Hama with Heimdall. If the two really were equivalent, one suggested, then the legitimacy of the spelling was questionable. Shouldn't it be 'Heimir', not 'Hama'?

Now, that was far too subtle and academic for me to answer. But 'Heimir' immediately made me think of 'Alzheimer', a name now inextricably associated with memory problems.

I thought about my dream and the knowledge within it that my memory of the toll-collector's face was being lost in the time between his image hitting my retina and that information passing up my optic nerve to the brain.

This is a 'god' of memory, I said to myself. A spirit who can interfere with the laying down of short-term memory so it never becomes long-term memory. A spirit whose Norse name is actually found within that of Alzheimer!

As I mentioned some pages back, I've never been able to verify this. But I believe it is true, given the preternatural accuracy of the rest of the dream.

There were several more alarming aspects to this discovery, however. As I read about the monstrous wave, I found that, according to the myth, a longship rode its crest. This ship, captained by the trickster Loki and manned by the giants of the north, was made of the fingernails of the dead.

Now Viking warriors, as they prepared for battle, clipped their nails. If they then died, they would contribute as little as possible to the construction of this ship. When I was twelve-years-old, I compulsively bit my fingernails down until they bled. I even knew why: I was afraid that, if I were run over by a bus and killed, no one would think to trim my nails. I wasn't actually afraid of being run over by a bus—only that, if I were, my nails wouldn't be as short as possible.

Light-bulb moment. I'd been trying to delay the coming of Ragnorok—just as the Vikings did! As I realised for the first time how much the dream had infiltrated my waking life, I wondered if I'd ever seen the ship-made-of-fingernails helmed by Loki. The nightmare was, after all, a regular occurrence with many slight variations. As I puzzled over the possibility, an interior voice suddenly spoke: 'No need to worry about that,' it said. 'We got rid of all those memories. They were too terrifying. So we dismantled that bit of the dream. It's been taken apart. It can never be retrieved.'

I was stunned. Who on earth was '*we*'?

Whoever it was, one thing was certain. I was complicit with the spirit of forgetting operating in my life. God had told me: 'It has rights you cannot even begin to imagine.'

I was starting to realise some of those rights came from my own participation—my agreement—with the process of forgetting.

I haven't often heard from that interior voice. I'm not sure that I can identify it, except to say that one of its jobs seems to be to alert me to spiritual danger. But it's definitely not the 'voice' I associate with God or the quiet nag of conscience. It's only made its existence known a few times but, on one of those, it roared at me.

It was in the late 1980s when it happened. I'd gone to a conference on fantasy at the University of Queensland which emphasised the academic side of the genre. One of the speakers was the science fiction author, David Lake—who, at that time, was also a professor of English. In his speech, he commented on his recently published novel, *The Changelings of Chaan*, comparing and contrasting it in philosophy and world-view to *The Chronicles of Narnia*. One remark he made was so provocative and struck me so forcibly that I wondered about it for years afterwards. It was this: 'Lewis doesn't use shapechanging in any of his work because, as a Christian, he views mankind as the highest of all possible lifeforms. It would be inconceivable for Lewis to have written something like T.E. White's *The Sword in the Stone* where the boy, Wart, undergoes a number of transformations including becoming a fish and a squirrel.'

As I thought critically about this statement, it dawned on me there wasn't a single Christian writer I knew of who'd used shapeshifting—that is, a genuine change of form as opposed to a merely illusory disguise—in any story. In addition as I considered using the notion in a story of my own, a sense of revulsion came over me.

Now I believed that I didn't think of humanity as the highest of all possible lifeforms in the universe and neither—in my view—did Lewis.[27] *But maybe*, I thought, as I pondered my revulsion, *maybe deep down I really do see mankind as some sort of pinnacle. Maybe I'm kidding myself. Was it possible,* I wondered, *that David Lake was entirely right? Perhaps I could have a go at writing a short story with real shape-shifting in it.*

That was when the roar occurred. 'DON'T EVEN THINK ABOUT IT!'

I jumped.

'DON'T BE RIDICULOUS, HAMILTON!' the voice bellowed. 'Lewis did it for personal reasons.'

I was astonished. How could the voice possibly know that? 'What *personal* reasons?' I demanded.

'It's too difficult to explain,' the voice replied. 'And yes, you do have the same personal reasons, but you wouldn't understand them at the moment. But don't worry—in ten years, you will.'

In retrospect, I realise how naïve I was. Still, after this bizarre conversation, I set about asking aspiring Christian fantasy writers of my acquaintance this question: 'Have you—*would* you—use a shapeshifter in a story?'

I explained what David Lake had said and asked for a thoughtfully-considered answer, not an off-the-cuff one. The responses varied. Some people said 'no', some people said that, while they hadn't, they couldn't conceive of a reason not to—but, it transpired, no one had.

And ten years later, I knew why. Because the concept of the shapeshifter comes from the myths of Scandinavia and one of the main words for it also means *familiar spirit.*

Complicity in covenant-keeping by inaction is one thing; though ignorance isn't bliss. But complicity in covenant-keeping by use of the active imagination is re-affirming the covenant of your ancestors for yourself.

Instead of revoking it, you re-inforce it. You provide a pathway for possession instead of merely oppression.

Had Lewis known about the spiritual connotations of a shapeshifter? I believe that, even if he didn't know consciously, he had the knowledge deep in his heart. Christians, like Jack Lewis, instinctively draw a line when it comes to shapeshifting, skinchanging and human metamorphosis. Buddhists, like David Lake, recognise the oneness that is inherent in such transformations but don't consider there's any problem with it.

Oneness however is the essence of covenant. And covenants with Ziz and its allies stand in the way of a covenant with God. How can He—the very embodiment of the Way, the Truth and the Life—be one with us when we're one with a spirit that tears truth apart and rips life to shreds?

How can He be one with anyone who has an ancestral covenant with the guardian of the rainbow bridge? The bridge that in Finland was Linnunrata, *the path of the birds*, and which features in Chinese and Japanese legend as the bridge of magpies?

We *know* Ziz. We might not know we know it, but we do.

Janus. Llyr. Leir. Lear. Heimdall. Hama. Heimir.

All names under which Ziz, the spirit of forgetting, can hide. There are many more.[28] So how can we spot their disguises? A strong clue is an association with doorways, gateways, beginnings, endings, openings, bridges, piers, ports and waves.

Heimdall, like Janus, is a 'god' of bridges. Heimdall, like Llyr, is a 'god' of seawaves.

None of them are exactly equivalent to each other within their respective mythologies—Roman, Celtic and Norse—but they have sufficient in common, it seems, for the spirit of forgetting and madness to slide between them.

'Trust me,' the toll collector had said within the dream. 'I'm an old friend of your family.'

Scary thought. Scarier still that, as I look back into the emotion at that point in the dream, I sense the toll collector's sincerity and genuine concern.

But the 'old friend of your family' bit makes sense now I know about name covenants. My surname is Hamilton. I'm convinced it derives from the same source as 'Hama', and thus 'Heimdall'. Thus there was a dedication within my name to a god opposed to the 'I AM' of the Bible.

Binding any spirit or trying to cast it out while a covenant exists with it is a futile exercise. It may even be counter-productive. In the case of the spirit of forgetting, it's what Jude calls an 'angelic majesty' so we need to be very careful not to overstep our authority.[29] Both Jude and Peter advise us in cases like this not to deal with it ourselves but to say: 'The Lord rebuke you!'

It's in ignoring this directive of these two apostles that many believers get smashed, mutilated and torn apart. Without consulting God, we try to exercise authority that we assume we have. '*Behold, I have given you authority to tread on serpents and scorpions, and over all the power of the enemy, and nothing shall hurt you.*' (Luke 10:19 ESV) This is our 'proof text' for the widespread belief that Jesus has granted us authority over Python and Leviathan, Ziz and Rachab—all the spirits of the threshold.

But this verse has been ripped out of context. It was spoken over disciples who *had just* passed over their threshold. Our problem is that we can't pass over the threshold into the space where we have this authority because these very spirits are going all out to stop us.

That's why we need a strategy from God. That's why we need to be aware of the schemes, tactics and agenda of the enemy. So that when God sends us a warning about a particular spirit, we don't waste our efforts trying to counter the wrong thing.

Ziz doesn't operate the same way as Python does. Python is a constrictor; Ziz is a raptor. It wants to tear our memory to shreds.

Its purpose is very simple: healing of body, mind and spirit comes through forgiveness and/or repentance. But if you can't remember what sin you've committed, you can't repent of it. If you can't remember what sin has been perpetrated against you, you can't forgive.

And though you may not recall the trauma you've experienced as a conscious memory, it will come out some other way. I didn't remember the longship made of the fingernails of the dead but I chewed my nails until the cuticles bled.

A woman my mother and I were ministering to brought up the possibility of incest. She remembered being terrified as a four-year-old of going to a park with her father. She had been told by a counsellor that sexual abuse had obviously occurred. However that did not gel with her memory of her dad; and in addition she mentioned that he had quite naturally brought up the subject of the park a few years previously. He revealed how much he loved taking her out and trying out different shots with his new camera. And as he brought out the photographs, she had a hard time reconciling the twinkling eyes in her bright four-year-old face with the remembered terror.

Then we recalled she'd made a comment earlier in the ministry: her mother had absolutely no memory of her life between the ages of three and seven. It was obvious. Something terrifying had happened to her mother around four years of age. Her mum might not have had the slightest clue as to what occurred to blank out those years but the epigenetic memory had passed down a generation to emerge as panic related to going to a park.

As Mark Wolynn points out, memory of trauma is never lost. It just emerges some other way.

When it comes to trauma, the brain is a very effective filing system. It doesn't actually store memories of traumatic events. It simply keeps a file noting the location in the body where the memory has been tucked away for safekeeping.

It does this for an intensely practical reason: we all want to avoid any recurrence of a similar trauma in the future. We also want to pass on to our descendents any knowledge that will help them avoid it too. So we become highly sensitised to particular smells or sounds, tastes, colour combinations or movements—because they are locked into us as sensory data associated with the initial trauma.

A particular scent may make me nauseous because it reminds me of a traumatic moment in my life and I instinctively go to high alert. Now this is of course a great faculty, if my traumatic incident was a gas explosion. But not so great if I can't stand to be around my boss just because he wears the same signature brand of cologne as a childhood abuser.

The human body contains its own pair of 'watchers'. Armed with the sensory information of past trauma, these sentinels are constantly on the alert to prevent recurrences of the event. They are the amygdalae, a pair of almond-shaped structures in the brain. Each amygdala processes stimuli from the external world and then connects that flow of information with the internal systems governing emotional reactions. The amygdalae have the reputation of being principally associated with fear.

However, the amygdalae are also involved in screening out the overwhelming tsunami of sensory data that bombards us every single second. They're like a pair of gatekeepers at a busy entrance who are trained to ignore the ordinary and notice only the abnormal. Now for their effective operation the amygdalae require access to traumatic memory. So they are connected to the process of recall as well as that of decision-making. They are also involved in memory consolidation. Long-term memory regarding life events or matters of learning is not formed instantaneously. Details of the event are slowly assimilated into long-term storage and it is the amygdalae that help to regulate this consolidation.[30]

Spiritually, I believe that God has revealed a part of His divine purpose in creating the amygdalae—simply through their shape. They look like almonds and, in fact, they derive their name from the Greek for *almond* or *tonsil*.

The connection between *almond* and *watching* is found in Scripture, at the beginning of the prophecy of Jeremiah:

> *The word of the Lord came to me: 'What do you see, Jeremiah?'*
>
> *'I see the branch of an almond tree,' I replied.*
>
> *The Lord said to me, 'You have seen correctly, for I am watching to see that my word is fulfilled.'*
>
> Jeremiah 1:11–12 NIV

Now the first time you come across this, it's baffling. It doesn't seem like a riddle. The pun that exists in Hebrew doesn't translate into English, so it makes no sense initially. In fact, it seems like nonsense. However, 'shaqad'—the Hebrew word for *watch*—is a pun for 'shaqed', *almond*. In actual fact, while we differentiate between 'shaqad' and 'shaqed' with different vowels, it is an artificial imposition of modern times. They are identical words in Hebrew.

The connotation of the word 'shaqad', *watching*, is more than simply to be *on the lookout*, it's *to be wakeful, to stay awake*, or *to be alert*. This is a lyrically appropriate description of the almond tree—traditionally it is the first to 'wake up' after winter in Israel and bring forth blossoms. It's a signal on the threshold of spring as the year passes from one season to the next.

But there are other words for *watcher* in Hebrew. In discussing the mezuzah, we looked briefly at 'shomer', *guardian*, from the word for *watchtower*. Just as the mezuzah is the watcher on the threshold of a house and the almond tree is the watcher on the threshold of the seasons, we could consider the amygdalae as threshold guardians when it comes to the body.

Sometimes these guardians become so activated by fear, they can't switch off. They are permanently on high alert, even when they don't really need to be. As a consequence, there's no possibility of relaxation or rest. The words of Scripture seem a mockery: '*You can go to bed without fear, you will lie down and sleep soundly. You need not be afraid of sudden disaster... for the Lord is your security*.' (Proverbs 3:24–26 NLT)

At this point, when we can't relax or get a good night's sleep because we fear the recurrence of a traumatic event, an opportunity arises for the various threshold spirits. Ziz can tempt us with the thought that there is so much solace in forgetting. 'If only I could forget all that happened...' is a wish that invites both Python[31] and Ziz to become active in our lives. 'I just want to forget this ever happened...' is a desire that opens the door to an agreement with Ziz.

Because ultimately, it relies on the spirit of forgetting as a source of comfort and denies that place to the Holy Spirit, the Comforter.

And because forgetting is tearing truth apart, we've slammed the door on Jesus—the Way, the Truth and the Life.

Prayer

A reminder: I strongly recommend that all the prayers in this book are read through carefully before being prayed aloud with intentionality. If you feel a check in your spirit from the Holy Spirit about any aspect of the prayer, then heed it. Put off the prayer until you receive permission from God.

It is vitally important to recognise that prayer is about relationship with the Father. It is not intended as a formula. The prayers in this book are meant to be guidelines to help you realign yourself with the holy Trinity; they are nothing in themselves; they are meant as a starting point, not an end in themselves.

Transformation is only possible as you hold onto the hem of Jesus' prayer shawl and ask Him to mediate before the Father for you. In the end, it's all about Him!

El Elohim Yahweh—*Mighty One, God, the Lord*—I come to You and ask You to remember me, to call me to mind, to look upon me and help me remember You.

Mighty One, You told me to do so much more than write and speak of Your goodness. You commanded me to teach the next generation to love You with their whole heart, mind and spirit. Lord, my children have a God-shaped hole in their hearts. Lord, I repent of not reminding my children of Your goodness, and of not taking the opportunities to instil in them a knowledge of the blessing that comes from obeying Your commands and the consequences of turning away from You. Please forgive me and fill me and my children with the balm of Your Holy Spirit, so that You will be glorified. Remind us all of who You really are.

Father God, I acknowledge my inability to relax and rest. I admit the many times I have lain awake at night fearing the unknown—afraid of imagined dangers. I have sought out many false refuges to comfort me, when in truth You should be my first and only refuge. Father, I know that fear is basically having faith in an evil that hasn't happened yet. Even so, I have chosen it over Your safe and secure protection. I repent of my failure to trust You—*Mighty One, God, the Lord.*

Please forgive me.

Abba Father, I am conscious of the many times I have allowed Ziz to shred my mind, confuse my brain and scatter my spirit. It seems as if it tore my memory into a thousand pieces and threw the fragments to the four winds. I allowed Ziz into my life—thinking that forgetting was a comfort, a desirable luxury. Abba, I failed to value one of Your most precious gifts—memory. Forgive me and gather together the scattered pieces of my memory, *re*-member them out of their dismembered state and restore them to me.

Father, You assigned me as a watchman to my community. I see now that I failed to honour You by fulfilling this aspect of Your calling over my life. Instead, I succumbed to the deceptions of Ziz. I fell for its distractions and ruses, and became caught up in a trap, partly of my own making. Open my eyes, Father so that I can become the person You designed me to be at my conception. I pledge to honour You and You alone. Please help me fulfil this vow.

Father God, I repent of taking the easy way out by lying and saying that an offence did not hurt and did not matter. I repent of quickly overlooking the dishonour heaped on me and of falling in with the plan of Ziz to forget it—instead of asking Jesus to accomplish His forgiveness through me.

Father God, I acknowledge today that 'out of mind' is *not* 'out of sight': that traumatic memory is stored somewhere in my body, even if my agreement with Ziz blocks my access to it.

Today, Father, I come out of agreement with Ziz and its lies and come into agreement with Jesus who is the Way, the Truth and the Life and. I ask You to heal me. Help me, Father, for Your name's sake. Amen

4

The Mezuzah of God

The lure of forgetting is often almost irresistible. It's a simple, appealing answer to trauma and conflict.

The Buried Giant is a novel by Kazuo Ishiguro. The press release accompanying his award of the Nobel Prize in Literature for 2017 says this: 'The themes Ishiguro is most associated with are: memory, time, and self-delusion... In his latest novel, *The Buried Giant*, an elderly couple go on a road trip through an archaic English landscape, hoping to reunite with their adult son, whom they have not seen for years. This novel explores, movingly, how memory relates to oblivion, history to the present, and fantasy to reality.'

The story in fact throbs with references to Arthurian legend, tales from English folklore and the deeps of Celtic mythology, as well as modern Christian cultural clichés and odd bits of Jewish mysticism. It ebbs and flows towards a climactic confrontation between the determined young warrior, Wistan, and the doddery old knight, Sir Gawain. Wistan is on a quest to slay a dragon—the very same dragon that, before his death, King Arthur tasked Gawain with destroying. In his old age, Gawain seems to have lost his nerve and become prickly with pride.

The elderly couple accompanying Gawain and Wistan through a landscape shrouded in mist are troubled by continual memory lapses. They are on a journey to find their son though they can't recall where he lives or even what his name is. In fact, they can't even properly remember who they are. Dream-like fragments of past identity float into their thoughts but the pieces seem like illusions. How could peasants like themselves have ever been a princess or the 'Knight of Peace'?

It transpires that Gawain—who obviously should have won the medieval equivalent of an Oscar for his acting performance—was never entrusted by Arthur with slaughtering the dragon. He's its guardian. The mist seeping across the landscape comes from the dragon's breath. It's been enchanted by Merlin to cause forgetfulness and wherever it settles, it fogs and fragments the memories of both Saxon and Briton alike.[32] So that the 'buried giant' of *vengeance* will not awaken.

The price of peace is loss of memory.

Yet the loss is much greater. The world Kazuo Ishiguro depicts in *The Buried Giant* is one without truth. It's also without justice and—consequently—without mercy. Forgiveness isn't a possibility, because no one remembers who they are or what happened. Peace was intended to reign supreme but it doesn't. Amnesia does.

In Hebrew understanding, it is God's breath that gives life through the power of name. In *The Buried Giant,* the dragon's breath takes life through the power of forgetting.

As the story unfolds, it becomes clear that forgetfulness was a price people were willing to pay for peace after the fall of Camelot.

For many of us, this is how our story unfolds as well: forgetfulness is a price we are only too willing to pay for peace of mind. Reluctant to do the hard yards of forgiving or repenting, we take the bait dangled by the spirit of Ziz—the easy route of forgetfulness.

Alcohol, drugs, hypnotism, even kinesiology,[33] can be our preferred mode of helping Ziz accomplish its task. The fullness of life Jesus promised us is compromised whenever we swallow one of these baits—or any other. Because fullness of life is exactly what Ziz wants to steal from us.

Apart from its two appearances in the psalms of Asaph, 'Ziz' turns up for a third time in Isaiah 66:11. The Jewish sages do not list this as a reference to the spirit of Ziz. As far as I can tell, they see this instance as a word, not a name. So obviously they find a nuance in the text that escapes me. Nevertheless, I include this Isaiah reference for the sake of completeness: '*...you may drink deeply with delight from her glorious abundance,* zīz.'

Here 'zīz' is translated *abundance*, not *bird* or *moving herd*. Here again there are breasts, evoking the nurturing comfort of El Shaddai, because the full verse starts: '*you may nurse and be satisfied from her consoling breast*.'

Both the *consoling breast* and *glorious abundance* linked together in this verse belong to Jerusalem. She is the city of full life and dazzling delight.

This abundance is promised us for remembering God and turning aside from other gods. This abundance is promised us for teaching our children about God's saving acts—both in biblical history and our personal lives. This abundance overflows so heavily that we may have to put some into storage.

And perhaps this is why 'zīz', *abundance*, is associated with 'mezuzah', *doorpost.* A storage space in an ancient Jewish home was often a cavity beside the door. For civic buildings, storehouses were built into the wide gateways—right beside the mezuzah.

By the time of Isaiah, God's commands regarding the mezuzah were thoroughly rejected: '*You have put pagan symbols on your doorposts and behind your doors. You have left Me and climbed into bed with these detestable gods. You have committed yourselves to them.*' (Isaiah 57:8 NLT)

The threshold covenant was so completely defiled by this that God was exiled as covenant defender of His people. And so, because we reap what we sow, there was no abundance in store—just the makings of exile.

The Hebrew word for both *remember* and *memory* is זכר, zkr. It's also the word for *male* and for *memorial.* In Exodus 3:15, it's used as *name.*

Memory and name have been linked since the time of Babel. After the Flood of Noah, when people spread out over the earth, they said, '*Come, let us build ourselves a city, with a tower that reaches to the heavens, so that we may make a name for ourselves; otherwise we will be scattered over the face of the whole earth.'* (Genesis 11:4 NIV)

The Tower of Babel was built to 'make a name': to ensure that they would not be forgotten. According to the Jewish sages, one of the three motivations for building the Tower of Babel was that it would serve as a memorial to those who died in the flood.[34] Now, of course, there's nothing inherently wrong with building a memorial. However, to *make* a name is to usurp the work of God. God makes us regents over names[35] but the creation of names is His.[36]

Now we reap what we sow. It's a law as inextricably embedded into the spiritual realms as the law of equal and opposite reaction is within the physical universe. So God's decree as a just Judge on the Tower of Babel was always going to be about names and forgetting. 'Babel' is named for the confusion God brought about in the language of the builders,[37] yet behind that confusion is forgetting.

> *'Come, let Us go down and there confuse their language, that they may not understand one another's speech.'*
>
> Genesis 11:7 NAS

David Patterson comments regarding this verse: 'in the confusion which tears word from meaning, people lose their memory of what a *person* means. And when we forget what a person is, people die, violently and indiscriminately.'[38]

The tearing of word from meaning: how deep is this forgetting! How can we describe such estrangement? It's like separating water from wet.

And this rending began with the decision to 'build a name'.

It's my suspicion that God didn't just confuse the language but also caused people to forget their own names as well as that of others. In His words, '*Come, let Us go down and there confuse,*' the word *there* may also imply *name*. Both 'shem', *name*, and 'sham', *there*, are spelled שמ.

Perhaps this is why *man* and *memory* are the same word. It's no coincidence that taking away a name and replacing it with a number, as happened during the Holocaust, allows those in authority to forget the personhood of those in their charge.

Benjamin was nearly nine years old when he arrived at Auschwitz. Housed with other children and with dwarves who were all selected for medical experimentation, he was subjected to cobalt radiation and treated with barbarous cruelty. 'We were like caged animals,' he said, 'with no hope, no spirit.' One day, dazed by the operations and the medication, he moved too slowly as he was being taken to the laboratory. As an officer began to beat him, a woman tried to intervene. 'He's not well,' she said. The officer took out his revolver and shot her.

Benjamin never forgot. Years later, he changed his surname to Steiner to remember Ruth Steiner, the woman who died for this moment of kindness.[39]

When we treasure others, we cherish their names. But when we forget names—forget them spiritually, that is—we stop seeing people as beloved of God. We see them as less than human. And in doing so, we cease to be truly human ourselves.

We don't make a name for ourselves by building a heaven-high tower; we learn what destiny and calling is already enfolded within our names by running to the strong tower found in the name of the Lord.

Martin Niemöller was filled with dread and loneliness as he made his way from his prison cell to a courtroom to be tried for treason against the Nazi state. He'd already spent seven months in solitary confinement and knew his sentence was a foregone conclusion. As he was escorted through an underground tunnel, he heard a low whispering echo of a voice repeating the same set of words. Eventually he realised it was his guard murmuring in an undertone and speaking from Proverbs 18:10—'*The name of the Lord is a strong tower; the righteous runs into it and is safe.*'[40]

Niemöller later said it was one of the most uplifting, unforgettable moments of his life. He doubted that the guard, whose face he never saw, ever realised what his action meant and what the courage and peace it had imparted to his prisoner.

Babel: a tower that was built to make a name and ensure a memory. Keep this in mind: don't forget that this first of all towers was about both name and memory. And those three things—tower and name and memory—are entwined more often than you'd suspect in the Scriptures. Sometimes their mingling is a disgusting mess and sometimes, as when Jesus gets hold of the three of them, it's a spectacular and majestic tapestry.

But before looking closely into all that, let's go to some threshold moments in the Scriptural record. The last of the prophets to write in Hebrew were Haggai, Zechariah and Malachi. They are believed to have been contemporaries around the sixth century before Christ. Of them, Zechariah is the only one to have made any mention of a vision of angels.

He is thus last recorded person in the Old Testament to have had an angelic visitation. The first recorded person in the New Testament to have an angelic visitation was also named Zechariah—though he's better known to us by its Greek variant, Zachary. In either case, Hebrew or Greek, the name means *God has remembered*.

Last of the old, first of the new, these Zechariahs were prophets on a threshold. And note: naming is so important in this story of 'God remembering' that He reserved it to Himself. God watched over the name He had chosen for the forerunner of the Messiah; He guarded it by silencing Zachary's tongue.

Zachary and his wife Elizabeth[41] were childless. A Levite priest, he received the call for a once-in-a-lifetime[42] opportunity: to offer prayers in the Temple at the altar of incense. There, perhaps in the same location that his namesake, Zechariah, was murdered,[43] he saw an angel who revealed that he was about to have a son and instructed him to name the child 'John'. When Zachary began to question this, he was struck dumb. He only regained his speech when the boy was born and he wrote on a tablet, 'His name is John.'

One of the signature clues within Scripture that an event is a threshold moment is the appearance of an angel. Angels and thresholds go together—regardless of whether those thresholds are physical ones or spiritual ones. From the angels at the gates of Eden to the angel who rescued Peter from prison and left him just after the city gates; from the angel who appeared in answer to Daniel's prayer to the angels who terrified the Roman soldiers at the tomb of Jesus; from the angel who appeared to Mary to tell her she was invited to become the mother of the Messiah to the angels who rebuked the disciples after the ascension of Jesus—all of them, every one, appears at a physical gateway or at a time when a spiritual transition is occurring, that is, when a divine door is opening or closing.

Angels and thresholds go together.

Mezuzot and thresholds also go together.

Like the mezuzot attached to doorposts, Zachary and Zechariah were effectively living memorials. A mezuzah, a sign of remembrance at a gateway, is situated right where a guard would be posted. In this, a mezuzah resembles a watchtower—because this, too, is where a guard would be posted.

This connection between a mezuzah and a watchtower is brought out in the iconic letter ש, traditionally decorating the mezuzot of today. As mentioned previously, the ש is regarded as an abbreviation of 'shaddai', which in turn is considered to be an acronym for **Sh**omer **D**altot **Y**israel, meaning 'guardian of the doors of Israel'. Shomer, however, as we have seen, is derived from the word for *watchtower*—and embedded in it is 'shem', the word for *name*.

Here again we have this deep connection between towers, memorials and names.

Why does God so carefully guard names? Perhaps because, without them, we are denied access to our calling. A name is the power to propel us into our destiny.

There's a Jewish story similar to the tales of Peter at the Pearly Gates. In this variation an angel guards the entrance to heaven. His task is to ask one very simple question. If the soul wanting admittance can give the right answer, the gates will be opened wide. But if not, the soul will be turned away.

The question is this: '*Who are you?*'

Behind this story is a profound thought about the nature of identity and memory. When we were conceived, God breathed into each of us a soul just as He did for Adam (Genesis 2:7). Because the word for *breathed*, 'nashamah', has an embedded 'shem', *name*, Jewish sages consider that God creates souls by naming us. In a whisper of love, He breathes a name into us, defining both our identity and our destiny.

So, if we have walked in that calling during life, we will remember our name and be able to answer the angel's question. But if we have turned aside from our calling, we have effectively forgotten who we are. We won't remember our true name when confronted at the gates of heaven and asked for it. We will be like the people of

Babel: scattered and lost, because we wanted to make a name for ourselves instead of trusting God to guard and protect our names for us.

The highlight of a charity fundraiser I was involved in was to be the auction of photographs and memorabilia autographed by different celebrities. Some of the more valuable items were securely stored by members of the organising committee. As the time for the auction approached, I asked one of them to retrieve those items in her safe-keeping. 'But I've already given them to you,' she said.

She described in explicit detail when and where she'd handed them over, what I'd said, where I'd put them, who had been around at the time. I remembered nothing about receiving the items but I'd been so busy and distracted for several hours that it was quite possible the handover was exactly as she'd said. For the next twenty minutes, I made a frantic search, my heart racing, my mind falling apart with worry. I raced around, tracking down everyone who had manned the desk where the handover had occurred, to ask if they'd seen or moved the box of memorabilia I'd put behind it. No one recalled anything but that didn't mean much. It was easy to overlook an ordinary cardboard box.

Just minutes before the auction was due to start, I gathered the organising committee together so we could prepare a suitable public apology regarding the loss of the items. As we did, the woman who said she'd given them to me abruptly announced, 'I might still have them. I'll go and look.' She turned to me in accusation.

'I'd have remembered if you hadn't distracted me by asking questions.'

I was stunned. I was shocked on so many levels I didn't know where to begin to list them. For twenty minutes this woman had watched me dash around madly, tormented with anxiety. The thing that stood out for me the most as my heart rate returned to normal was this: she hadn't told a lie. She *genuinely believed* she'd made that handover. She had been able to describe the circumstances surrounding it in such high level detail that I didn't think to question her story.

It was a seminal moment.

After this incident, I started to take more notice when events like this happened around me. I eventually realised that there are people—not many, thankfully—who have a pathological inability to admit to a mistake. They cannot say 'sorry', even though they often believe they have.

They need to be right. Perhaps 'need' isn't quite the right word. It doesn't convey the utter urgency of the imperative to be right. Such people re-arrange history in their minds. Now memory is often unreliable but this goes far beyond a selective perspective on events: it is a deliberate tearing apart of truth so it can be re-organised to portray the person in the best possible light. I'm sure some individuals with this deep-seated need believe so fervently in their sanitised version of events they could pass a lie detector test.

Now behind this ability to re-arrange history and actually believe it to be true is a vow:

'I must always be right.'

'I am never wrong.'

'I refuse to accept that I am ever mistaken.'

However this vow expresses itself, it is a legal foothold as far as the spirit of Ziz is concerned. This spirit cannot access our lives without our complicity. It can empower our vows, making them stronger, but it cannot force us to make vows in the first place. It can tempt us to make those vows, and it can re-inforce the structures that come from them, but it cannot compel us to open the door to it in the first place.

Threshold spirits like Ziz are opportunists. They take advantage of vows like these that take root in our souls as a consequence of abuse or trauma experienced at an early age.

Often the vow is as simple as: 'I don't ever want to remember this.' Over time, given enough life wounds and painful episodes, Ziz can help us contrive a slight modification: 'I don't ever want to remember.'

There are of course many benefits to forgetting. And not all forgetting is bad. But when it takes the place of forgiveness or of repentance, we're in trouble. We've invited the Ziz, spirit of forgetting, to help us deal with our problems. And we've sent away El Shaddai, the Lord Almighty, the comforter and nurturer, the One who offers abundance and fullness of life.

The tragedy of cooperating with Ziz is that, after a while, we don't even know *that* we've forgotten, let alone *what* we've forgotten. This is why, as I said right at the beginning, it's my nominee for Hell's Most Efficient Employee.

The Jewish legend of Ziz tells us that one of its alternate names is Sekwi, the *seer* or *watcher*. This rare word is only found once in Scripture. It makes its appearance in Job 38:36 NIV—'*Who endowed the heart with wisdom or gave understanding to the mind?*'[44]

The word rendered as *heart* is 'sekviy'—an obvious variant of 'sekwi'. Besides meaning *seer* and *heart,* it also means *meteor*. Although it's been traditionally translated *heart* in this chapter of Job,[45] the immediate context of neighbouring verses features clouds, lightning, ice, frost and starry clusters. With these words surrounding it, perhaps it's better translated *meteor*. Particularly given the association of Ziz with the astronomical phenomena of eclipses.

Yet if 'sekviy' was rendered *meteor,* we'd miss all its psychological and spiritual aspects. The hidden relationship between *heart* and *meteor* perhaps explains the seemingly abrupt transition in Psalm 147 from verse 3 to 4 (NIV): '*He heals the broken-hearted and binds up their wounds. He determines the number of the stars and calls them each by name.*'

Binding the broken-hearted, counting the stars: then, in a flash, we're back with *name*.

It should not be unexpected. Name covenant and threshold covenant are inextricably associated. If there is one, then there is the other. They are invariably separated by six days. We underestimate how important our names are to these fallen spirits. Because our names are their targets.

If they can get our names, they can get our identities, our destinies, our callings and our souls.

> *And the Lord God formed man of the dust of the ground, and breathed into his nostrils the breath [nashamah] of life; and man became a living soul. [neshama]*
>
> Genesis 2:7 HNV

Both *breath* and *soul* contain the Hebrew word for *name*, 'shem'. When we try to create a memorial name for ourselves as mankind did at Babel, we reject all the aspects of name that God gives us: *soul* 'neshama'; *breath* 'nashamah'; and *light*—through *oil* 'shemen' and the *sun* 'shamash'.

God's original plan for memory-building was the mezuzah. This was initially the doorpost itself, before the word instead came to refer to the container affixed to the doorpost. Every time someone entered or exited a home or a city, they were directed by the presence of a mezuzah to remember God—to love Him and obey His commands. And if they did, they would prosper. There would be abundance.

There are hints that God's plans went beyond this symbolic reminder to also include living, breathing mezuzot. Zachary and Zechariah qualify here: they are the embodiment, in their names, of the promise that 'God remembers' and they are also prophetic 'types' of Christ as the Mezuzah of God.

Just before the first Passover: '*Moses called for all the elders of Israel and said to them, "Go and take for yourselves lambs according to your families, and slay the Passover [lamb]. You shall take a bunch of hyssop and dip it in the blood which is in the basin, and apply some of the blood that is in the basin to the lintel and the two doorposts; and none of you shall go outside the door of his house until morning.*' (Exodus 11:21–22 NAS)

Just before another Passover: '*Jesus knew that His mission was now finished, and to fulfil Scripture He said, "I am thirsty." A jar of sour wine was sitting there, so they soaked a sponge in it, put it on a hyssop branch, and held it up to His lips.*' (John 19:28–29 NLT)

Before the first Passover, the blood of a lamb was applied to the doorpost using a hyssop branch. At the latter Passover, wine—symbolic of the new covenant in Jesus' blood—was applied to the bloodied Lamb of God using a hyssop branch. The imagery could hardly be more explicit: Jesus *is* the Mezuzah of God.

He has fought the spirit of forgetting and won.

And when we go out, when we go in, wherever we are, we are to join in His victory and remember Him. He's the high tower we should run to in time of trouble or trauma. He's our Peace and our Passover. His is the memorial name and His Cross is the watchtower that achieved what Babel did not: it brought heaven to touch earth.

For three hours during the time He was on the Cross, the sun was darkened. Now a Passover occurs at a full moon, so a solar eclipse is out of the question. The moon is on totally the wrong side of the earth and cannot possibly pass in front of the sun. Besides a total solar eclipse lasts just minutes, not hours.

A lunar eclipse is quite possible—except for one thing. They don't occur during the daytime. So it's out too.

But something happened that day. When God rips up a covenant with death, He promises to inform us by an *un*natural event in the natural world. That event, so He decreed in Isaiah 28:21, will be as strange as the sun standing still. The normal laws of the physical universe will be momentarily suspended—or perhaps superseded—as this covenant is cancelled.

At the very beginning of this book I outlined the legend of Ziz: an eclipse-producing bird whose unfurled wings blot out the sun. Even this snippet of folklore points to Jesus, the Mezuzah of God. As He tore up the covenant with death—the ultimate forgetting—an eclipse darkened the land.

As He died, the veil of the Temple was torn in two.

But He wasn't done with the spirit of forgetting—not by a long shot. In fact, His death was just the beginning of its overthrow.

Prayer

Still another reminder: I strongly recommend that all the prayers in this book are read through carefully before being prayed aloud with intentionality. If you feel a check in your spirit from the Holy Spirit about any aspect of the prayer, then heed it. Put off the prayer until you receive permission from God.

It is vitally important to recognise that prayer is about relationship with the Father. It is not intended as a formula. The prayers in this book are meant to be guidelines to help you realign yourself with the holy Trinity; they are nothing in themselves; they are meant as a starting point, not an end in themselves.

Transformation is only possible as you hold onto the hem of Jesus' prayer shawl and ask Him to mediate before the Father for you. In the end, it's all about Him!

Yahweh, I recognise that the forgetting spirit is a real, powerful and cunning spiritual entity. Made even more effective because in addition to being the spirit of forgetting, it is so often the forgotten—the overlooked—spirit. It lies low and creates chaos because I do not know it is behind my confusion. Lord, from this day forward I resolve to be alert to the tricks of Ziz and to remember the chaos and confusion it has caused in my life. Help me, Lord.

Father God, Your way is so simple. Recognise — repent — forgive — reconcile — restore.

Ziz has said to me: Forget it all and never recognise, never repent, never reconcile—it is so much easier. Father, I have been in agreement with this and it's so wrong. I repent of following Ziz and believing that its way is the easy way. Forgive me and teach me to remember Your way is the only way to restoration with others and with You.

El Shaddai, I repent of having de-valued others. I repent of the times I have forgotten they also are loved by You, made in Your image and treasured by You. I am sorry I listened to the enticing voice telling me that others deserved my condemnation so I should forget Your principles of honour, Your 'golden rule' of treating others as I would like to be treated myself. I am sorry that I thought about other people in defiling ways and spoke dishonouring words about them.

El Shaddai, nurturing One, I am reaping the results of my own sowing. Help me. Heal me. Bind up my broken heart and help me to re-train my spirit and mind and bring them into alignment with the mind, heart and spirit of Jesus.

Yahweh, You breathed a name into Adam, a soul was created and human life on earth began. You whispered Your name for me and my soul was created and my life began. Forgive me, Yahweh, for dishonouring the person You made me to be. Forgive me for not listening to You and for ignoring and forgetting the value You place on me. Yahweh, I ask You to rescind any legal rights Ziz has to control me or to overshadow me with confusion and forgetting.

Today I tell it to be gone from my life. All invitations and legal rights are withdrawn. Ziz, may the Lord rebuke you.

Lord, may Your Holy Spirit enter the places where Ziz has been, and take up residence there. I invite you to find any pockets of forgetting that are holding out on Your healing and hold them up to the light and bring them to my memory.

I ask You too, through the blood of Jesus, to empower all the words I have spoken today and to make them manifest in my life.

In the mighty name of Jesus and with thankfulness for His memorial in the Cup and the Cross. Amen

5

The Hill of Government

God is a poet. He's a wordsmith. He spoke or—so some people believe—sang the heavens and the earth into being.

He's not a scientific rationalist. The universe He fashioned is fundamentally logical—however, He reserves the right to allow an unnatural thing in the natural world when He's doing things like breaking a covenant with death. Moreover He Himself is not limited by logic. If He were, He couldn't be both perfectly just and perfectly merciful—because, quite frankly, in the natural they cancel each other out.

God is not only a poet but we, as Ephesians 2:10 says, are His poetry. He breathed a soul into us through the tender whisper of a name.

I say all this by way of introduction to a radical concept: God is not first and foremost an etymologist. My contention is that, when it comes to applying the meaning of names in the lives of people, poetry is paramount—*not* the original or literal sense of the word. Yes, etymology is relevant, but it's far from the whole story.

Poetry makes connections through rhymes, puns and wordplay that don't bear up for even a second under scientific scrutiny. The Greek mindset baulks at paradox; the Hebrew mindset takes it in its stride. With a completely mechanistic worldview, it would be a struggle to persevere this far into this book. Because I've been using poetic connections constantly.

I want to be upfront about this because we're going to take a big leap sideways and look at some synonyms of 'zīz'.

Remember back in our discussion of Psalm 50 that 'zīz' was variously translated as *insects, animals, wild beasts, creatures* and *living things*? And remember too that I suggested the root meaning of 'zīz' was *lots of things moving to and fro*: basically coming down to things that swarm, flock, run around in packs or herds? Perhaps we could extend this to things that flow as they're stashed in abundance in storehouses—thus encompassing the secondary meaning as well.

Amongst the things that swarm are 'zebub', זבוב, *flies*. Jesus was accused of performing his miracles through the power of Baal-zebub, *lord of the flies*. This is a remarkable assertion because it puts Jesus in the company of Ahaziah, son of Ahab and Jezebel, who seems to have worshipped this Philistine god. Not long after Ahaziah became king of Samaria, he fell through the lattice in an upper room. Severely ill, he sent messengers to the temple of Baal-zebub in Ekron to ask the god whether he would recover. Elijah intercepted the messengers, rebuked the king and prophesied his death.

If we turn our attention from swarming things to those that run around in packs, we find 'zeeb', זאב, *wolves*. This is derived from 'zahab', זהב, *gold*. Apparently the reason for this relationship between the words for *wolves* and *gold* is because their fur, at least in the immediate region, is distinctly yellow in colour. DNA testing has revealed the Israeli wolf of today has interbred at some point in ancient times with the golden jackal, a member of the dog family.

Now remember my point that poetry is more important to God than etymology? I bring this up because I'd like to draw your attention to the name איזבל about which the prophet Elijah declared: '*Dogs will devour Jezebel by the wall of Jezreel.*'

Jezebel's name comes from the mystery rites of Canaanite religion. It's an unusual name in that it is actually a question. Perhaps the only other similar name is Michael, meaning *who is like the Lord?* Jezebel means *where is the Lord?* It was the cry of Canaanite worshippers gathered outside a cave as they enacted the sacred drama of Baal's annual return from the underworld.

But Elijah ignores that. In decreeing her end, he speaks as if the most significant part of her name is 'zeeb', *wolf.* He uses the word 'keleb', *dog,* but if wolves and dogs had interbred, the words would have been almost interchangeable. For the prophets, the burden of an oracle was to reveal how the destiny within a name would unfold—once an individual or a city had chosen to pursue the positive or the negative within their name. As they discern a pattern, they could warn of impending disaster and the need for repentance or they could encourage people to remain faithful.

Many prophetic utterances detailing events to come are based around a poetic vision of the names of places and people. Sometimes the root meaning of the name is significant, sometimes it's all about wordplay.

And speaking of wordplay, look at this: 'ezob', אזוב , the Hebrew word for *hyssop.*

The spirit of Ziz is the spirit behind Jezebel, queen of Samaria, wife of Ahab, daughter of Ethbaal, mother of Ahaziah and Joram, great-aunt of Dido of Carthage, and nemesis of Elijah the Tishbite.

To demonstrate this, it's necessary to show far more than the 'zīz'-'zeeb'-'ezob' connection; it's necessary to uncover evidence that points to her position as a threshold guardian.

You may wonder at this point why I've chosen to call the spirit of forgetting Ziz and not Jezebel? First I want to honour God's intention for memory. He might want to forget our sin but He doesn't—until we've dealt with it. Nor does He want us to forget it either until we've actually dealt with it. And we deal with it through recognition, forgiveness and repentance. Secondly, the name Jezebel is freighted with baggage. Unfortunately, as soon as it is mentioned in some Christian circles, there's an indecent rush to point fingers, make unholy accusations and bring forward insults and denunciations. The 'spirit of Jezebel' is a label all too easily flung at anyone a leader dislikes—particularly strong women, though increasingly it's directed at men. The tag is always offensive and derogatory; it is invariably meant as a term of dishonour.

Now Ziz must rub its monstrous wings in glee every time this kind of condemnation happens. Because while it personally doesn't gain any legal rights from dishonour, its ally Leviathan certainly does. They make a superb team—a dynamic and demonic duo of the utmost cunning.

Today, many churches and Christian organisations exhort their members to inculcate a culture of honour. Peter instructs us: '*Honour everyone. Love your brothers and sisters in the faith. Fear God. Honour the emperor.*' (1 Peter 2:17 GWT)

Unfortunately, in some circles, 'honour' has been understood to mean undivided loyalty to the senior pastor or highest representative in the hierarchy. If we turn our minds back to Rosella's efforts to ensure undivided loyalty in the cage, we might see the twofold aspect of this: feed the masses and use opportunistic murder.

And while physical murder is fortunately extremely rare, murder of reputation is on the other hand extremely common. And in places where the push for power is directed towards enhancing undivided loyalty, people often fear to speak up about problems because they've seen what's happened to others.

When a 'culture of honour' lacks mutuality—lacks any sense of the first part of Peter's exhortation, '*Honour* ***everyone***,' then it's merely another form of manipulation and control.

When a 'culture of honour' becomes a one-way street, then God's directive has been hijacked to serve a desire for an elevated status above that of other people. Whenever we build ourselves up by putting others down, no matter who we are, we set the scene for the reaping of a major putdown.

Some ministers object: 'But I'm anointed and appointed.'

So, as a matter of fact, was the anointed cherub we call 'Satan'.

Let's be clear about Jezebel before we go any further. And let me re-iterate: the spirit of Ziz, the spirit behind Jezebel, is the spirit of forgetting—a threshold guardian. It is an *angelic majesty* (2 Peter 2:10 *and* Jude 1:8). It is not an ordinary 'daimonion', *demon*, like those Jesus repeatedly cast out.

This is a critical distinction. It cannot be emphasised too strongly that we should never ever dishonour these spirits. Peter and Jude are in agreement that the consequences for doing so are extremely serious. The cautions that I outlined in the previous book in this series on Python are worth repeating here: there are warnings throughout the epistles of Jude and Peter about dealing with fallen angelic powers that many believers simply ignore. As I previously mentioned, I believe the spirit of Ziz is one of the 'exousia', *powers*, as is Python. The 'exousia' are entities that higher in rank than the principalities mentioned by Paul in Ephesians 6:12 and lower in rank than the world-rulers of the same verse.

Many Christians naïvely believe that all believers have authority over these powers. Actually what we have been given is armour to protect us from them, but the authority to deal with them only comes *after* we cross the threshold. This is exactly what Ziz is intent on stopping us doing: it doesn't want us to have authority over it, so it teams up with the likes of Python, Rachab and Leviathan to stop us. These spirits are not natural friends; they're natural enemies—but their fear of what will happen if we get authority over them brings them into a mutual alliance.

The issue of authority has been the cause of so much damage to believers in their walk of faith that it's important to get our thinking right on that matter.

First, the statement of Jesus upon which so much teaching about authority rests is: '*Behold, I have given you authority to tread on serpents and scorpions, and over all the power of the enemy, and nothing will injure you.*' (Luke 10:19 NAS) The next verse cautions the disciples against rejoicing that these spirits are subject to them. Both that and the phrase 'all the power of the enemy' tell us that these serpents and scorpions are high-level demonic entities.

The word Jesus uses for *authority* is 'exousian', from the same word Paul used to describe the angelic powers 'exousia' in Ephesians 6:12. We are given authority of that same high order—*once* we have passed the threshold.

Jesus had instituted a name covenant and a threshold covenant for His church *before* sending out these seventy disciples. (Luke 9:18–36) The significance of the timing tends to elude believers today. So does the existence of these two other covenants—which are independent of blood covenant. Without the threshold covenant, the powers that are arrayed in battle against us are simply impossible to defeat. Unless we can hold up an invitation from God, signed in the blood of Jesus, we are not going to be able to pass over the threshold into our calling and receive this authority. And if we think we get such an invitation the moment we're saved, it's time to think again. Saul of Tarsus didn't become Paul until about fourteen years after he fell off his horse on the Damascus road. This time period is fairly standard—it was close on fourteen years after Abram cut a blood covenant with God that he was invited to exchange names with El Shaddai and become Abraham.

Bottom line here: authority comes with faithfulness. We are entrusted with authority when we demonstrate we are willing to listen and obey God, not just in the crises of life but in the little things too. Because, when it comes right down to it, authority simply does not equal permission. We've been trained think the two are synonymous: that spiritual authority automatically confers divine permission. In fact, it's the other way around. If you seek permission from God and He grants it, you necessarily have any requisite authority. But when you use authority assuming it equals permission, it is far too easy to operate outside God's will.

This question of authority is particularly important when it comes to threshold spirits. I believe that Ziz is, like Python, Leviathan or any of their immediate allies, a spiritual potentate, not a foot-soldier. It belongs to that class of demons that both Jude and Peter call 'angelic majesties'. According to Tom Hawkins,[46] such high-level cosmic entities do not appear to desire embodiment in human beings, like 'diamonion' do. However, they may choose to seek embodiment for a particular purpose. When Jesus came down the Mount of Transfiguration after enacting a threshold covenant for the church, He encountered a boy with a demon. He *rebuked* the demon, it left and He told His bewildered disciples: '*This kind does not go out except by prayer and fasting.*' (Matthew 17:21 NAS)

Here we have Jesus modelling exactly what Jude and Peter encourage us to do: ask the Lord to *rebuke* this threshold guardian. Prayer and fasting make a difference—but even so they must be at the Lord's direction.

We are permitted to say, 'The Lord rebuke you,' to Ziz or to the spirit of Jezebel. We can also go directly to Jesus or the Father and ask Them to rebuke it. Can we say, '*I* rebuke you, Jezebel' as so many people do—or is that presumption?

We are not permitted to revile, abuse, insult, condemn, censure, despise or dishonour this spirit. The consequences for doing so are dire. Even fatal.

Many of us expect God to protect us while we violate His word. That is *not* what grace means. Grace is the power to keep His word, to hold on to Him against the odds, to follow His commands in the middle of the deepest pull to fling them aside. It is not a free pass to trample on what He has asked of us.

Now the fact that we are not to dishonour Ziz or any of its allies doesn't mean to say we should show it honour, either. But the same is not true for people. An attitude of dishonour for others is abhorrent to God: '*Don't rejoice when your enemies fall; don't be happy when they stumble. For the Lord will be displeased with you and will turn His anger away from them.*' (Proverbs 24:17–20 NLT)

It doesn't occur to us that, sometimes, the very reason God does not allow our cry for justice against an adversary to be fulfilled is because we have displeased Him with our gloating or contempt. '*Take delight in honouring each other*,' Paul admonishes us in Romans 12:10 NLT. The ESV translation goes further: '*Outdo one another in showing honour*.'

Now we need to be careful here: just as we are directed not to dishonour angelic majesties, but should not honour them either, we should be extremely cautious with our behaviour towards others. In honouring others, and in creating that mutual culture of honour that God delights to see, we nevertheless need to guard against the inveterate human tendency towards idol-making: we do not want to suddenly find that, having cleaned up our act in one way, we've made a mess in another. We don't want to elevate 'Honour' so it's a god.

Really honour is just part and parcel of the new command of Jesus: '*Love one another: just as I have loved you*.' (John 13:34 ESV) To truly honour others, even those we'd like to sneer at and slap a 'Jezebel' label on, we need to resolve to see them the way God sees them: beloved, delightful, precious in His sight, full of potential.

CS Lewis in *The Weight of Glory* says: 'There are no ordinary people. You have never talked to a mere mortal. Nations, cultures, arts, civilisations—these are mortal, and their life is to ours as the life of a gnat. But it is immortals whom we joke with, work with, marry, snub and exploit—immortal horrors or everlasting splendours.'

When we refuse to respect any aspect of God's creation, we do not treat Him with honour. We need to see the Jezebels of life as He sees them. And how exactly, you may wonder, is that?

Ahh! Scripture has several exquisite, hidden surprises on that score.

Jezebel was a Phoenician princess, the daughter of the expansionist king, Ethbaal of Tyre and Sidon. Ethbaal—also called Ithobaal I—was a priest of Baal who seized the throne by killing his predecessor.

He was the great-grandfather of Dido, founder of Carthage.[47] His economic and spiritual influence throughout the region was pervasive; his strong diplomatic ties with Omri, the ruler of the northern kingdom of Israel, were reinforced through the marriage of their children: Jezebel and Ahab.

Omri was a commander of the armies of Israel who was elevated to that throne after the civil war following the murder of the king by Zimri, a fellow officer. A strong man who perpetrated much evil, Omri does not appear to have been as ruthless as Ethbaal. When he wanted a piece of land for his palace, he bought it. Ahab followed this example when he wanted to expand his palace—and Jezebel's solution of killing anyone in opposition, no doubt learned from her father's methods in seizing the throne, does not seem to have occurred to him.

Omri acquired his site from a local landowner, Shomer. The hill in question came to be named after him: Samaria.

Eventually this was to become the name of the people of the region—the Samaritans.

Shomer means *watchtower*; thus 'hill of Samaria' is *hill of the watchtower*. But note: embedded in Shomer is 'shem', *name*. The spiritual motivation behind Omri's ambition is clear. His palace-building programme is driven by the same forces as those that inspired Babel—this is about the building of a tower to make a name.

In the Jewish legend about the construction of Babel, the tower rose so high that it took an entire year for a brick to be passed up the human chain from the kilns at the bottom to the brick-layers at the top. If a brick fell from the tower, a great cry of lamentation went up. But if a human fell from the tower, no one even paused in their work. Life had ceased to be precious, to be worth guarding, to have meaning.

Just so, with Jezebel's coming to Samaria, life ceased to be precious, to be worth guarding, to have meaning. Her father had been a priest of Baal and she brought his religion with her. This included child sacrifice offered to Baal Melqart and ritual prostitution in the name of the goddess Astarte. No doubt she would also have participated in ritual of Baal's return from his imprisonment in the underworld kingdom of death, accompanied by the cry, '*Where is the Lord?*' This, after all, was the origin of her name.

The defilement that the gods of Tyre and Sidon brought to Samaria spread quickly. In the brief summary of Ahab's reign, the rebuilding of Jericho is mentioned, along with the child sacrifice that was entailed: '*In Ahab's time, Hiel of Bethel rebuilt Jericho. He laid its foundations at the cost of his firstborn son Abiram, and he set up its gates at the cost of his youngest son Segub, in accordance with the word of the Lord spoken by Joshua son of Nun.'* (1 Kings 16:34 NIV)

The spirit of forgetting was already at work in Israel long before Jezebel's coming. But her advent caused a whole new level of falling away to take place.

Falling.

It's a subtle thread in Jezebel's story. Just three verses after her first mention in 1 Kings 16:31 comes the comment about the rebuilding of Jericho. For about five centuries it had remained uninhabited until Hiel began his renovations.

Ahab and Hiel, despite the English transliteration giving a contrary impression, have a common root. Hiel is said to come from 'ach' and 'el', thus meaning *brother of God* and Ahab is thought to come from 'ach' and 'ab' meaning *brother of my father*.

The mention of Jericho is apparently placed to foreshadow how Jezebel would die. Just as the walls of Jericho were renowned for falling at a trumpet blast, so Jezebel would fall from the walls of Jezreel. And while there is no trumpet blast in the natural world—at least that we know of—to accompany her end, there seems to have been one in the spiritual. The word used for Jezebel's fall from the window—helped by a hefty shove—is 'shamat'. There are more than a dozen words for *fall* in Hebrew, but the choice is significant: it's the only one related to 'shemittah'.

In *The Mystery of the Shemittah*, Jonathan Chan reveals God's ordinance: every seven years—at the moment when the new year begins with a trumpet blast—all debts are wiped out. A huge economic release was to occur: property returned to its original owners, slaves set free, liabilities over inheritance cleared, debt cancelled. The Shemittah, *release, let fall, drop*, was a threshold moment designed to reset the balance in society. No doubt a faithful few fulfilled the command but it's doubtful it was ever enacted on a large-scale basis. This is clear from the God's proclamation through Jeremiah:

> *I said: 'Every seventh year each of you must free any fellow Hebrews who have sold themselves to you. After they have served you six years, you must let them go free.' Your ancestors, however, did not listen to Me... Recently you repented and did what is right in My sight: each of you proclaimed freedom to your own people. You even made a covenant before Me... But now you have turned around and profaned My name; each of you has taken back the male and female slaves you had set free... You have forced them to become your slaves again. Therefore this is what the Lord says: 'You have not obeyed Me; you have not proclaimed freedom to your own people. So I now proclaim "freedom" for you,' declares the Lord—'"Freedom" to fall by the sword, plague and famine.'*

Jeremiah 34:13–17 NIV

As shown here for ancient times and also by Jonathan Cahn in his analysis of wealth redistribution over the last century, God is fierce in His insistence on the Shemittah.

It's no coincidence that, just as a new dynasty started, Jezebel had a 'shamat' onto the very field she stole from Naboth. Her body was torn apart by dogs, just as Elijah had prophesied: '*Dogs will devour Jezebel by the wall of Jezreel.*' (1 Kings 21:23 NIV)

This prophecy is, to my mind, based on the poetry of her name. Elijah didn't base his words on the actual meaning of Jezebel—*where is the Lord?*—with its overtones of Phoenician religion. Rather he heard the nuances of its central syllable, 'zeb', and spoke of *wolves, jackals, dogs*. And perhaps of 'azubah', *forsaken*.

In other subtle echoes, he reminded her of the defeat of her priests at Mount Carmel. Naboth's vineyard—the Hebrew word is 'kerem' and is related to 'Carmel'—would be the scene of her final defeat. She would be *torn apart*, 'kircem', a rhyming word.

He invoked the same principle that Paul later did: '*Do not be deceived: God is not mocked, for whatever one sows, that will he also reap.*' (Galatians 6:7 ESV) Knowing that Jezebel had influenced people to forget God's injunction to redeem firstborn children, not sacrifice them to Melqart, Elijah realised she would reap the consequences of forgetting. Since forgetting is dismembering truth, dismemberment must follow. This judgment was reinforced by her actions in actively pursuing the dismembering of truth through bribing witnesses to make false accusations against Naboth.

Ziz, however, as the spirit of forgetting and also of dismemberment of truth, uses false allegation in more than one way. It can tempt us to falsely accuse others. Not only is truth torn apart but we dishonour others—this invites retaliation by Leviathan. On the other hand, Ziz can project defilements over us, causing others to level such serious false accusations that we are deprived of our rightful 'inheritance'—anything from our reputation to a career or property. Such defilements are perhaps hinted at in Deuteronomy 15:9 which links a refusal to keep the divine shemittah to an 'evil eye'. Jesus in Matthew 6:23–24 links the 'evil eye' to serving the god of money which in the first century was Melqart.

The spirits, Ziz and Python, operate differently. Python will try to constrict, intimidate and tempt to divination; Ziz will try to devour, rip and falsely accuse.

And just as Jezebel allowed the worship of Melqart, whom the Israelites called 'Moloch', to become established through child sacrifice, so the spirit of Ziz will, if you manage to get over the threshold, try to slay your newborn destiny. It's a baby-killer. And it doesn't matter to it whether the infant is spiritual or physical.

This is why it's so important to come out of agreement with it. Our desire to forget is not the only issue—trouble can also arise from unanswered false accusations before the throne of God. The satan has brought a case to God, a tissue of lies and misconstructions, but that case has never been dismissed—because it has never been answered. Our inaction has allowed falsehood to be uncontested and truth concealed.

We can be complicit with Ziz in many ways. All need to be repented of; all need to be renounced. Its tactics are invariably about temptation to:

1. forget in order to avoid the pain of trauma, instead of asking God to help us remember without pain
2. agree to rip truth apart, either through forgetting, revision of history or false accusation
3. dishonour, so we can be attacked by Leviathan
4. leave false accusations unanswered in the court of heaven
5. make a name for ourselves through our towering achievements
6. sacrifice our newborns, whether those children are spiritual or physical
7. tolerate the actions of Jezebel

But Jesus, the Mezuzah of God, is not only the Way, the Truth and the Life but also the Shemittah who releases us from the power of Ziz.

Death is a threshold transition for us all. But when Jezebel died, it was a spiritual threshold for the kingdom of Israel as well. With her fall, dynastic change occurred. The threshold is subtly indicated in the story-telling when it is reported her blood splattered the wall and she was trampled by the horses of Jehu. Blood, in combination with trampling, indicates refusal of covenant.

Stumbling, falling, dashing your foot, trampling, *stepping on* rather than *passing over* the blood on the cornerstone—all these words and phrases are ways of expressing a rejection of covenant. Jehu's action symbolises his refusal to covenant with the gods served by Jezebel. Belatedly, he remembers to honour her body—but this too is appropriate, since we are called first to sever any covenant with the spirit of forgetting but, secondly, not to dishonour it in the process.

In the Book of Revelation, Jezebel is described as one who seduces the saints of the church. Specifically she's charged with misleading '*My servants into sexual immorality and the eating of food sacrificed to idols.*' (Revelation 2:20 NIV)

While seduction is on this spirit's agenda, so is forgetting. We can only be seduced when we deliberately rip up the twofold testimony of God's truth—that of His Word and of His Spirit within our conscience. We have to shunt one or both of these aside.

Remember the story of Rosella who picked so daintily at the blood feather, as if relishing a fine delicacy? Michael Youssef points out that 'delicacies' were originally food that had been offered first to the gods. Ancient people ate the leftovers of such sacrifices as a means of identifying with the gods.[48]

The issue, as always, is covenant. In a sexual encounter, you become *one* with another person. When you eat food that identifies you and the god as *one*, a covenant is forged. These two things—immorality and eating 'delicacies'—are not the only ways we can covenant with Ziz: they are simply representative examples.

The spirit of Jezebel wants us to forget the call of God and covenant with another god—sometimes just re-affirm that covenant with another god who has been an old friend of our family for generation upon generation.

The call on our lives can only be truly fulfilled when we cut covenant or re-affirm covenant with Father God, the one whom Jesus of Nazareth called 'Abba'. Our covenants with Ziz, its allies or any other unholy spirit must be severed.

We are called to stand on the hill of government in our lives and there declare, as the people of Israel did at Shechem, that we choose God.

Shechem is the location where Jesus met the woman at the well. He asked, in effect, for far more than just a drink of water: He asked for the government of her life as well as the lives of everyone in Samaria.

Shechem is the location of Joseph's tomb. He left instructions that his bones were to be disinterred when the people of Israel left Egypt and re-buried at Shechem.

We see in Joseph a strong contrast with Ahab. In fact, we perhaps see in Joseph a model of the man Ahab was meant to be if he had broken his covenants with the gods of his wife.

Both Joseph's father-in-law, Potiphera, and Ahab's father-in-law, Ethbaal, were pagan priests. Ethbaal was a priest of Astarte, and Potiphera a priest of the sun-god. However, given Asenath's name, it is probable her father also worshipped the war-goddess Anat, who was often paired with Astarte. Also given that Ahab built a temple to the sun-god in Samaria, it was certainly influenced, if not financed, by Ethbaal. Thus both Joseph and Ahab had fathers-in-laws who worshipped the same god and goddess.

Was Ahab meant to be the 'Joseph' of his age? Was he meant, like Joseph, to prepare for the coming of a famine? Instead he blamed Elijah for prophesying the drought! Was he meant, like Joseph, to have saved lives? Instead he allowed that mantle to be taken up by his high steward, Obadiah.

Both Ahab and Joseph built and fortified cities—Ahab constructed an ivory palace while Joseph constructed storehouses. In both their times, the priests of the land received an allotment of food from the royal house,[49] enabling them to live luxuriously even during times of great hardship.

Joseph's bones came back to the land of his inheritance—Jacob bequeathed Shechem to Joseph on his deathbed. '*And to you I give one more ridge of land than to your brothers, the ridge I took from the Amorites with my sword and my bow.*' (Genesis 48:22 NIV) The Hebrew word 'ridge of land' is Shechem. Perhaps it's no coincidence Ahab was killed by a shot from a bow.

Yet 'Shechem' is not merely *ridge of land*—it also has overtones of *shoulder* and *government.* Throughout Scripture, the number associated with government is seventy. Jacob has seventy 'sons', though strictly they are descendants. Ahab's seventy sons, effectively executed by Jehu (2 Kings 10:1), may also actually be his descendants. Another man associated with Shechem who had seventy sons was Gideon. Perhaps it's no coincidence that one of Ahab's significant failings was in government—not only did he dispense unsanctified mercy in war but he also was careless in allowing his seal to be used without permission by his wife to murder Naboth over an inheritance. In contrast, Joseph carefully tested his brothers as he allowed divine mercy to operate through him and there's no record of anyone ever using the seal Pharaoh gave him without permission.

Shechem was in the territory of Ephraim and the hill of Samaria in the tribal allotment of Manasseh: both these tribes descend from Joseph. Ahab has an unusual name. Often suggested as meaning *uncle* or more accurately *brother of my father*, its original sense seems lost—though poetically, it is related to ''ahab', *love*. No commentator seems willing to hazard the possibility it actually means *I am the brother of my father*, indicating Egyptian influence on marriage customs. The Pharaohs often married their sisters and thus fathered their own nephews.[50] In fact, rabbinic lore passes down the tradition that Asenath, wife of Joseph, was actually his half-sister Dinah. If that seems odd, remember this was centuries before the giving of the Law. Abraham had married his half-sister Sarah and, hundreds of years after Joseph, the father of Moses, Aaron and Miriam married his aunt.

From this comparison, we can see who the people we're tempted to call 'Ahab' are meant to be. And that God wants us to pray to call forth the 'Joseph' in them.

In his prophetic, pattern-analysing masterpiece, *The Paradigm*, Rabbi Jonathan Cahn links the spirit behind

Jezebel to abortion. I would add that this spirit, being the spirit of forgetting and dismembering, allows our society to be content with compartmentalised, disparate thinking. On the one hand, our government foots the bill for IVF treatments; on the other, it pays for abortions. In my home state over a recent ten-year period, 204 children survived such abortions simply to be left to perish.[51]

The increasing commodification of children—as a product to be bought or sold,[52] discarded or abused—is a sign of forgetting.

The increasing grooming of children from an early age to awaken their sexuality long before its natural time[53] is a sign of forgetting.

The increasing use of children in irreversible gender-change experiments is a sign of forgetting. Nearly a century ago, we would have called such treatment 'eugenics'—and it was forgetting then, just as it is now. Such forgetting led to Nazi justification for the Holocaust.

Some children who are diagnosed with gender dysphoria may simply have Asperger syndrome—it is often accompanied by confusion about gender. Aspergers, I believe, is heavily influenced by the spirit of Python.[54]

Remember that story about the angel who guards the gates of heaven and who asks you your name? As a society, we're not only forgetting our own names—and their significance for our identity and destiny—we're also forgetting our children have names. We're forgetting God breathes a soul into each of us at conception by whispering a name. In forgetting how precious and wondrous a child is, we tear apart the truth of divine naming. We rip identity to shreds, we devour destiny, we deny the calling of the child—and, more than that, we reject God's assignment for us as a family and the mission He has given our ancestral line to complete.

We give Ziz our undivided loyalty and sacrifice our children to forgetting. Just as Jezebel asked for undivided loyalty through the offering of children to Moloch.

Names are the carriers of these assignments and missions—they are the power to summon us into our calling, to remind us of the unique identity God has given us, to propel us into our destiny.

We find the Hebrew word for *name*, 'shem', hidden in many exotic places. It's concealed in *breathed*, 'na**sham**ah', which describes God's action in creating a soul, thereby indicating God creates souls through naming. It's embedded in the word for the *heavens*, 'ha**sham**ayim'—suggesting that God didn't merely speak *words* to create the universe, He spoke *names*.

It peeps out of the related words, '**sham**at', *fall*, and '**shem**ittah', *release, drop, let go*. Given that 'mittah' means *bed*, perhaps we could speculate that at least one sense of 'shemittah' is the bedding down of a future name covenant. This word, 'mittah' derives in turn from another for *lying down, inclining, leaning, turning away*.[55] In theology we often refer to the rebellion of Adam and Eve as 'the Fall' and, while there are many Hebrew words that could be used for this, perhaps 'shamat' with its sense that *falling* is *turning away from your name* has the right resonance. In Revelation 2:22, Jesus speaks to the angel of the church of Thyatira warning that He will throw the self-proclaimed prophet, 'Jezebel', onto a sickbed because she had been given time to repent but refused. Those words *throw* and *sickbed* in combination suggest 'shemittah': *release*—but, for Jezebel, not a joyful one. Those who tolerate her, as Ahab once did, will come into *tribulation, persecution, affliction* or *distress.* The Greek word, 'thlipsis' for *tribulation,* derives from *constriction, pressure, being hemmed in* and is therefore highly suggestive of being delivered into the hands of the spirit of Python.

While we're examining the poetics and wordplay built into 'shemittah', let's note two rhyming syllables. The first is 'emeth', אמת *truth*, which admittedly has a different 't' from 'shemittah'—a 'tav' not a 'tet'—but the sound is very similar. The same variation in 't' occurs in 'mitt' or 'meth' meaning *death.* The word is probably the base of our word, 'mortgage', *property put up as security for a loan or agreement,* which comes originally from a French word for *death writ* or *death pledge.* If a shemittah were to be kept as God ordained, a mortgage—*a death pledge*—would die every seven years at the sound of a trumpet blast. But when we forget to enact the shemittah as God intended, to release captives, to forgive our debtors, to set truth free, then our forgetfulness brings back to us those things we have failed to do for others. Truth can't set us free because we've forgotten it, so we remain in prison, enslaved and disinherited. Perhaps our ancestors have even suffered exile and we're still living with the outworking of that.

The shemittah has, as Cahn points out, a mysterious connection to eclipses—but he is unable to clarify what it is. It occurs on a threshold—at the moment when the old year of the Jewish calendar ends and the new begins. It is the start of a ten-day preparation time for Yom Kippur, the Day of Atonement—a day that in Scripture is girded about with questions of name and identity. It was when the Pharisees asked John the Baptist if he were the Messiah. Two years later, again on Yom Kippur, Simon confessed that Jesus was the Messiah and received the name Cephas.

In both these instances, six days later a significant threshold arrived—in the first case, Jesus performed his first miracle, and in the second, Jesus was transfigured on a high mountain. In fact, in my view, He was transfigured on the same mountain the Book of Enoch states is where 'the Watchers'—a class of fallen angels—descended to earth before they took wives from the daughters of men.[56]

Watcher, as we have seen, is one of the nuances of 'shomer', *the guardian who defends the threshold*. It is another curiosity in our collection of words featuring 'shem', *name*, and it has overtones of doorways, boundaries, liminal spaces and transitional zones. However 'shomer' also means *watchtower* and is the basis of the placename, Samaria.

Now when it comes to names, nothing is ever simple. Besides *watchtower, watcher, sentinel* and the like, there's another assumed root of Samaria: 'shamor', the modern word for *fennel*. The Greek word for *fennel* is 'marathon' which, as Arie Uittenbogaard points out, is possibly related[57] to Hebrew 'mara' and 'mor', *myrrh*—the fragrant oil used by Mary to anoint Jesus' feet and by Nicodemus after His death on the Cross.

Let me repeat my statement: God is not an etymologist. He's a poet. Lexicons will tell us bluntly that such words as 'sham', *here*, and 'shem', *name*, while having *absolutely* identical spelling in Hebrew (though we distinguish them in English with a different vowel), have nothing to do with each other.

The word 'hashamayim', *heavens*, is understood by some Jewish people in less than currently approved scientific thinking. Rashi, the famous medieval scholar, thought it could be translated *fire in waters*. Because the word for *fragrant oil* is 'shemen', some sages consider that another translation is *perfumed waters*.[58] Far more obvious to me personally is *the sea of names*.

If the heavens are sweet-scented, then spiritually speaking so are doorways—at least they should be if Jesus is reigning there as Jesus is the Shemittah, the Mezuzah of God, the Chief Cornerstone, the Capstone, the Gate of the Sheep and the Key with the government upon His shoulder. The armour of God is blissfully fragrant[59] and it is specifically designed for crossing thresholds. Moreover, the names of certain herbs and flowers are traditionally associated with doorways.

Rhoda, meaning *rose*, was the name of the servant-girl in charge of the gate at the time of Peter's miraculous release from prison. With a touch of high comedy, she leaves him knocking while she rushes to deliver the wonderful news that he's alive and well and on the front step. It's a delightful interlude where two names, Peter and Rhoda—both threshold-evocative—clash over the issue of their respective callings. The rose had long been associated with gateways through the phrase, 'rose of Sharon'. Sharon is a name associated with the Hebrew word for *gate*.

Rosemary is a name combining 'rose' with its nuance of *gateway* with 'mary', *myrrh*. Or perhaps *fennel*. If, as Arie Uittenbogaard suggests, 'mary' is related to *fennel* and derived from 'shomer', *watchtower*,[60] then the name Rosemary has a sense of a *watcher at a gateway*. Spiritually therefore the name points to a mezuzah: the symbol of memory.

Isn't this just perfect for the herb rosemary which, for centuries, has been reputed as enhancing memory? 'Rosemary for remembrance', so said Shakespeare, drawing from English folklore. And research has confirmed exactly that: a 'rosemary room' filled with the diffused scent boosted memory retention by 15%. Peppermint tea also helped but chamomile was deleterious.[61] Some researchers found that actually sniffing the essential oil of rosemary increased memory retention by 75%.[62]

While we're on the topic of herbs and essential oils, it should come as no surprise to discover that myrrh increases attention, alertness and clarity, as well as helps memory retention. Likewise fennel increases alertness and clarity. Fennel seeds and almond—and remember that almond in Hebrew is 'shaqed', the same as the word for *watching*—are regarded as a great boost for memory.

All of these words—myrrh, rosemary,[63] rose of Sharon,[64] fennel, almond—have names that are inter-connected, not by any standard etymology but by a lyrical relationship to watchers, watchtowers, gateways and thresholds.

Yet clinging to them also is the distant legacy of that first tower at Babel—the memorial which was meant to make a name for its builders. These herbs and plants are memory-enhancers; some of them have become common names; they all point spiritually to the mezuzah, the doorpost that was sprinkled with blood on a twig of hyssop. And yes, no surprise here either! Hyssop is used for the restoration of memory loss.

In fact, the Hebrew word for hyssop, ''ezob', derives from a root meaning *from times of old* or *ancient times.* According to Chaim Bentorah, it is associated with a recall of history: in other words, he maintains, *with bringing up memories.* He suggests that David asked the Lord to cleanse him with hyssop in Psalm 51, where he brings his sin with Bathsheba before the Lord, because 'operation of cleansing is to remove all memory of what was once there and allow you to start fresh or new. Learning from your past mistakes or others learning from your mistakes and not repeating them eases one's guilt over his past errors.'[65]

The ancient sages, he points out, spelled ''ezob' as Aleph (*God*), Zayin (*protecting what is precious*) and Beth (*home* and/or *heart*).

This kind of remembering actively learns from sin: aiding forgiveness, repentance and renunciation, thus cleansing the heart and beginning anew.

I believe this is why God created so many plants to help us with our memories. Because, as well approach the threshold into our calling, we have such a formidable enemy in Ziz, the spirit of forgetting, that we need all the help we can possibly get.

Gold dust rained down, night after night, in a small country church. The glory of God was so immanent and the gold dust so thick, so the pastor testified, that he had to sweep it up after each service. In an effort to get the church building spotlessly clean, he'd simply throw all the dust outside into the waste bin.

The first time I learned of this story—from a minister well-acquainted with the pastor—I wondered, 'Is that all? The glory of God appears in tangible, visible form and the pastor's regular, ongoing daily reaction is to sweep it up and dump it?'

I couldn't understand the story, which was supposed to illustrate the glory of God, because it raised so many questions and didn't provide an answer to any of them. The minister's reaction seemed so bizarre—at least to me. Had he no curiosity about the quality of the gold? Or even if it was gold and not pyrites? Or possibly some new element, not yet found on earth? Why didn't he take photographs or videos? Didn't he really believe in what he was experiencing? Or did he feel that, if he subjected the dust to chemical analysis, he was in some way questioning the holiness of God? But, then, what did throwing out the gold signify? What did that say about God's glory in our midst?

The pastor himself couldn't explain his actions—and didn't really make an effort to. But to me, with my ever-present question, 'Why?' lurking just below the surface of my thoughts, I felt he should have at least made a guess regarding his own motivation.

This story has lurked in the back of my thoughts under the label of 'inexplicable' for years. It sat on the same shelf in my mind as 'biting fingernails down to the quick in case you get run over by a bus'. But recently, I wonder if it's about forgetting.

In Hebrew, *gold* is 'zeeb'.

But 'zeeb' is also the word for *wolves* and, by association and inter-breeding, *dogs, hyenas* and *jackals*. In addition, it's got a sense of *packs, herds* and *groups of moving things.*[66] It's related to 'zebub' meaning *flies* or *swarms of moving things*. This suggests that 'zeeb', *groups of moving things*, is cognate with 'ziz', which also means *groups of moving things.*

Basically 'zeeb' is one step—perhaps one and a half—removed from 'ziz'. *Gold* is therefore a neighbour of *forgetting*.

And, being a neighbour, is a rain of gold dust God's way of giving the strongest possible proximity alert that the spirit of forgetting has taken up residence next door? This may not be so in every case, but it is certainly true in some instances. At one time, towards the turn of the last century—notably a threshold time—along with gold flakes floating down during worship services, gold fillings started spontaneously appearing in some people's teeth.

What does 'gold teeth' mean? To me, gold teeth isn't something I automatically associate with El Shaddai. I don't recall gold teeth being mentioned anywhere in the Bible. Which is not to say that God, for His own purposes and for His own glory, couldn't or wouldn't miraculously provide gold fillings. However, I instinctively associate gold teeth with a particular threshold spirit. It's that same spirit who appeared in my dreams, claiming to be an 'old friend of the family' and whose face I could see but never remember. Heimdall, so the Norse legends go, has gold teeth and his hearing is so keen he can hear grass grow in the field and wool on sheep.

This is the guardian I personally associate with forgetting. Moreover he has a name variant which happens to be found within 'Alzheimer'. So, despite the disbelief of sceptics, I don't find it at all curious that many people who claimed to have received a miraculous tooth replacement realised at a later date that they'd simply forgotten their dentist has supplied the gold filling.[67] This combination—gold teeth together with forgetfulness—does not suggest the God of the Bible, but another god entirely.[68]

Or rather it does suggest the God of the Bible—at least in one way. It suggests to me that El Shaddai was giving churches all over the world early warning that there was something they'd forgotten. His timing was significant—so many of these manifestations of gold occurred in 1999. Just as the world was approaching a new millennium, so was the church. And, on the threshold, sentinels were lining up to guard the passage of time from the twentieth century to the twenty-first. They are the same watchers who take their stations when it becomes obvious that we are about to step into our destiny and take up our own calling.

On the approach to the threshold we'll encounter Ziz, the spirit of forgetting. Then, on the threshold itself, the spirits of Python and Rachab, the constrictor and the waster.

Should we somehow make it over the threshold, we'll find Leviathan the retaliator bounding up to greet us.

So, back at the turn of the century, I believe God was allowing these creative miracles as a sign to remind us that we'd forgotten to keep watch over the millennial threshold. Unless the church, His Body, prayed strategically across that transitional period, then we'd allow ungodly cosmic entities to make covenants at tactically beneficial moments. And let me assure you, those angelic majesties took advantage of a church that was largely asleep—and ignorant. I count myself as one of those snoozing away.

One of the other manifestations of the time that accompanied the gold dust and gold teeth was laughter. This, even more than the gold, is indicative of *threshold*. However, as a sign, it's much more ambiguous. Laughter, in Scripture—especially as it relates to threshold events—is sometimes positive and sometimes negative. And when it's positive, it's very, very positive. And when it's negative, it's very, very, very negative.

The first time Scripture records laughter occurring on a threshold is when Sarah, at the entrance to the tent, hears God say she's about to have a child. Her laughter actually occurs during a threshold covenant. Abraham had received three visitors—God accompanied by two angels—and he'd invited them into his tent for a meal. Such hospitality in ancient times constituted a threshold—or cornerstone—covenant; the participants automatically had covenantal expectations and obligations towards one another.

God challenged Sarah about her laugh and she denied it. Apparently she found it absurd to think that, at her age—decades past menopause—she'd find herself pregnant.

A similar kind of laughter happened when God's angelic escort were rescuing Lot from Sodom. Lot tried to warn the young men betrothed to his daughters of the impending destruction—and they laughed dismissively. Again, their reaction seems to be about the absurdity of what they're hearing. And again the laughter occurs *during* a threshold covenant.

In both these instances, the Hebrew word for *laughter* comprises three letters: tsadi-het-qoph, צחק. This is transliterated as 'sahaq'—or 'tsahaq' (or, in the past, 'tzahaq' or 'zahaq'). Here is the foundation of the name, Yitshaq, meaning *laughter*—in English, Isaac.

Now the reason I'm making a fuss about the spelling is because there's a similar biblical word meaning *laugh*. It too is transliterated as 'sahaq' but it's composed of different Hebrew letters: shin-het-qoph, שחק. So it rhymes with tsadi-het-qoph, צחק.

This is significant because laugh-with-a-shin isn't directly threshold-associated but it does have many such indirect poetic nuances. First there are some words we've met before: 'shaqed', *almond*, and 'shaqad', *watch*. Then there are words that are explicitly threshold-related like 'mashaqoph', *lintel*, and 'shaqoph', *framework of a door*.

In addition, there is 'nashaq', *armed, armoured* or *weaponed*, which may not initially appear to be threshold-related. However in Ephesians 6:10–18 where Paul describes the Armour of God, it's clear this protective gear is designed for the specific purpose of crossing thresholds and warding off spirits like Ziz and Python. Seven puns about entrances exist in this passage. Just a few examples: the Greek word for *shield* is also used for *door* and the word for *darts* is actually *threshold* itself.

However, 'nashaq' has other meanings. It means *kindle*. It means *kiss*—an integral part of extending hospitality to a guest as they crossed the threshold. Jesus points out the shortcomings of Simon the Leper as regards a threshold covenant when He says: '*Do you see this woman? I came into your house... You did not give Me a kiss, but this woman, from the time I entered, has not stopped kissing My feet.*' (Luke 7:44–45 NIV)

It seems this dual meaning of 'nashaq', *kiss* and *put on armour*, was influenced by 'hashaq', *be closely attached*. Armour, after all, has to be attached closely to the body to be effective. And perhaps the third meaning of 'nashaq', *kindle*, was influenced by another sense of 'hashaq', *love* and *delight*.

God is a weaver of words. He's a poet. He doesn't ignore etymology and root origins by any means but it's not His principal way of outworking the destiny of individuals or peoples or places. Look at His promise to Jerusalem: '*Never again will you be called* "The Forsaken City" *or* "The Desolate Land". *Your new name will be* "The City of God's Delight" *and* "The Bride of God".' (Isaiah 62:4 NLT)

The contrast of 'azubah', *forsaken*, with 'hephzibah', *delight*, isn't a perfect rhyme. It's a poetic device called assonance.[69] Take note of these two words, 'azubah' and 'hephzibah':

the first has a syllable very close to 'zeeb', *wolf* or *gold*, encoded in it. And the second is almost as close.

But back to laughter. Other words belonging in the same grouping of laugh-with-a-shin are 'sehoq', *jest*, and 'mishaq', *deride* or *scorn* or an *object of ridicule*. Perhaps we might also include 'shaqah', *drink*, in this category since, when we're talking alcoholic drinks, mockery, laughter and contempt abound.

There's also 'shaqaph', variously translated *overhang* (thus probably derived from *lintel*), *look out, lean over, overlook*. It's used to describe Jezebel immediately before her death. She *looks out* of a window at Jehu. Perhaps in this instance 'shaqaph' is chosen to evoke far more than simple looking. Does it reflect the manner in which she's looking? Does it imply she's laughing at Jehu? Certainly her words are provocative, subtly hinting that Jehu is going to kill himself by the end of the week.

However, there can be no certainty she's mocking him.[70] The same word is also used to describe the eunuchs who look out the window and respond to Jehu's call to throw Jezebel down. Still, *throw* is definitely a threshold word in this instance: it's 'shamat', from which 'shemittah', *drop, release* is derived.

This is the same word Jonathan Cahn relates to the moment of transition from the old year to the new—the threshold of fresh beginnings with its release from all debt and bondage and its return of inheritance. I believe 'shemittah' is implied in Jezebel's fall onto the very land she stole from Naboth: this threshold moment meant the rightful heirs could resume their inheritance.

So what do we make of laughter? When it pertains to a threshold, it can—as in the story of Isaac—be the start of God's fulfilment of His promises to us. Or it can—as in the stories of Lot and his sons-in-law, Jezebel facing Jehu, Samson being mocked by the revellers in Gaza and Abner suggesting a bit of suicidal fun to Joab at the Pool of Gibeon—be the prelude to lots of spilt blood.

I'm not sure which spirit influences threshold laughter: Ziz or Leviathan. When God questions Job about Leviathan, He links it with threshold laughter and birds. (Job 41:5)[71]

Originally created to frolic in the deep, Leviathan was a fabulous sea creature massive enough to provide a feast for the entire company of Israelites after they'd crossed the Red Sea and were journeying into the desert (Psalm 74:13–14). I agree with Arthur Burk that its spiritual counterpart is supposed to bring unstoppable joy and bubbling delight to our lives.[72] However it's a fallen seraph, so the laughter it provides is twisted to derision and ridicule.

Laughter on a threshold is therefore decidedly ambiguous. That's why our relationship with God is important: so we can ask Him to clarify whether or not it's a counterfeit of joy. Happiness is not joy, and laughter that does not give strength is not joy either. For, as Nehemiah 8:10 NIV says, '*the joy of the Lord is your strength.*'

Once upon a time at the beginning of this century, I read through a wide range of books by many different authors while trying to discover what the nursery rhyme *Hickory*

Dickory Dock actually meant. Sometimes you can sense there are spiritual dynamics you're missing and, as I read *The Bone People* by Keri Hulme, *Borderliners* by Peter Høeg and others including the series starting *Time Stops for No Mouse* by Michael Hoeye, I tried to uncover what was really behind the pattern of time and towers and climbing mice.

I really loved Hoeye's charming series starring the reticent watchmaker mouse, Hermux Tantamoq. One of the beautiful things about the early stories was that, as he went to bed each night, Hermux would mention what had happened during the day that he was thankful for. His gratitude was inspiring. And so obvious. I felt a little embarrassed that a fictional mouse should point out such a hole in my relationship with God. And so I began the habit of thanking God for things at the end of each day. At first it was hard. It sounded awkward and clumsy, but after a while, persistence brought a natural flow to it all. And after a while, I didn't wait until the end of the day anymore. I started to take opportunities as they arose.

In retrospect, it was the act of routine thankfulness that turned my life around. James Merritt in *52 Weeks Through The Psalms* points out that there are four things God wants from us. And it's absolutely no coincidence that these four are revealed in Psalm 50, the very same song where Ziz is first mentioned by Asaph.

God wants us to be *thankful*.
God wants us to be *truthful*.
God wants us to be *trustful*.
God wants us to be *thoughtful*.

We should be *thankful,* Merritt notes, for the goodness, grace and guarding of God. We should be *truthful,* bookending our lives with honesty and integrity, even when there's a price to pay as a result. We should be trustful, believing that God will indeed come when we call upon Him '*in the day of trouble*'. (Psalm 50:15 ESV) and we should be *thoughtful,* opening our lives to God for a complete makeover, a transformation of our day-to-day behaviour that glorifies Him in all we do.

Ann Voskamp in *One Thousand Gifts* remarks that remembering is an act of thanksgiving. More: that remembering with thanks builds trust and faith. Here we have the reason why does Ziz not want us to remember: because if we were to do so and give thanks in everything, in all circumstances good and bad, we would have joy. We would be followers of Jesus, acting just as He did in that moment on the night before He died when, knowing the death that was before Him, He took bread and 'eucharisteo', *He gave thanks.*

Nestled within that word, 'eucharisteo', Greek for *thanksgiving,* is another word: 'charis', *grace.* And hidden within 'charis', like a sweet kernel, 'chara', *joy.*

Deprived of remembering, we are deprived of the opportunity to burrow into joy—that wondrous fruit of the Spirit that is our strength. The secret of overcoming Ziz is joy, and we receive joy through thanksgiving—as we express ourselves in grateful words and expend ourselves in grateful actions.

Prayer

Yet another reminder: I strongly recommend that all the prayers in this book are read through carefully before being prayed aloud with intentionality. If you feel a check in your spirit from the Holy Spirit about any aspect of the prayer, then heed it. Put off the prayer until you receive permission from God.

El Shaddai, I come into Your presence by faith and I repent of the many times I have disrespected others, dishonoured them and failed to think and act with dignity in reaction to them—forgetting that my body is a temple of Your Holy Spirit and I defile that temple through my unholy thoughts and actions. Forgive me, Father, for dishonouring You through my disrespect for others.

I repent of the many times I thought my adversary to be a 'Jezebel' or an 'Ahab'. I repent of speaking that name out with condemnation instead of praying to call forth your design in them. Forgive me for overlooking the 'Joseph' you wanted to cultivate in those I thought of as 'Ahab'. Forgive me for mocking them, laughing at them, ridiculing or disparaging them.

Forgive me also for dishonouring the spirits of Jezebel, Ahab and other powers, principalities and world-rulers rather than simply asking You to rebuke them.

Your Word tells me to '*take delight in honouring each other.*' I have not honoured others with delight and joy. I ask for Jesus to come beside me and empower my repentance. I have expected honour but not been willing to extend it. Again I ask for Jesus to come and empower my repentance. Forgive me for thinking that this portion of Your Word is irrelevant and I can ignore, disregard, overlook and forget it. I am sorry, Father. I am reaping what I have sown. You ask me to judge actions with discernment but not people with condemnation. I have failed You. Forgive me and, through the power of the Cross and the power of the blood of Jesus, give me the grace from this day forward to 'take delight in honouring each other.'

Father, I resolve that my every thought, word and action will be a signpost to Your Kingdom of joy, honour and respect in the world. Send Your Holy Spirit to help me and Jesus to guard my mind. In His name. Amen

6

Watchkeeper Bride

In the previous book in this series, there's a long rambling appendix on *The Silver Chair*, a children's fantasy adventure by CS Lewis. I consider that classic novel to be an exemplar showcasing the many and varied tactics used by threshold spirits to stop you achieving your calling. Although the plot reaches its dramatic climax with the confrontation of a character representing Python, the heroes face persistent attacks by the spirit of forgetting as well.

Unfortunately Jill and Eustace are complicit with this spirit, since they fail to obey the Great Lion's direction to repeat the 'signs' daily and thus commit them to memory. Peter Harris wrote to me on reading the appendix in *Dealing with Python* and pointed out an aspect I'd overlooked in the story. The castle of the giants, he suggested, represents an insidious tactic of these threshold spirits. 'My theory,' he said, 'is that there's *always* a HOUSE of Python, full of creature comforts, conveniently located right before the door we're meant to go through.'

He rightly identifies this 'House of Python' as a false refuge. Castle Harfang in *The Silver Chair* was set in a freezing cold wilderness, right on the doorstep of the ruins the heroes needed to penetrate. Only under the ruins could they find the lost prince—the reason they'd been summoned into Narnia in the first place. It was snowing a blizzard outside Castle Harfang, but inside were warm beds, food feasts, Puddleglum's favourite tipple—in the same square black bottle only twenty times as big. The castle was a gilded cage the heroes couldn't escape while they were being fattened for the feast.

If they'd diligently followed the 'signs', they wouldn't have wound up as prisoners about to be served up as a dainty morsel to satisfy the palates of their ever-smiling captors. Harris was reminded of the line from the song, *Hotel California*, about being able to check out anytime but never being able to leave.

The insight is profound. When we're complicit with Ziz, we're not going to remember how to avoid the 'House of Python'. And it's not just Python we have to worry about; all the threshold spirits gather in our false refuge to dine on us.

And, although we expect God to come to our rescue, He doesn't respond to our desperate cries for help. But why would He? When what we really want is for Him to remove Python's constriction over our lives while leaving us snuggled up to the consolations and comforts of Python's residence. We want God to be our protector and defender but we have no intention of moving out of the enemy's camp while there are still advantages to living there.

We're like Cain, warned by God that sin is waiting on the threshold, wanting to be our master. '*If you do well, will you not be accepted? And if you do not do well, sin lies at the door. And its desire is for you, but you should rule over it.'* (Genesis 4:7 NKJV)

But instead of mastering sin, we allow it to be our master. Instead of using the grace God makes available to us to conquer our enemy, all too often we use grace as an excuse to make a truce with one of the threshold spirits. The trouble is that our adversary can see such an agreement as legal grounds for dispossessing us.

Cain, the tiller of the soil, was angry when the sacrificial offerings of his herdsman brother, Abel, were accepted and his were not. Now let's take a moment to note their vocations: a tiller of the soil and a herder of animals. One was a grower and the other a drover. As a consequence, by simple virtue of their occupations, they pursued totally different ways of life—Cain was settled, Abel was a wanderer.

It's clear that, when Cain sinned, he lost the very thing that he prized most: his settled, grounded life. He suffered great distress when God pronounced his punishment: to wander the earth. Yet, despite his misery and his claim that his punishment was more than he could bear, Cain was simply required to do the very thing his brother once did: to move from place to place. He reaped what he had sown—in killing the wanderer, he became a wanderer.

Cain was dispossessed. And, because God had warned him that he needed to master sin, he sabotaged himself. His complicity with the guardians of the threshold, the spirits lying in wait at the door, led to a double tragedy. He murdered his brother. And, in doing so, he lost both his inheritance and his calling.

As I write this chapter, a scandal has rocked Hollywood. Several very influential movie stars and executives have been accused of rape, sexual harassment and misconduct—in one case, nearly seventy actresses have come out with harrowing stories about the same man which go back decades. In the ongoing blame game, an overlooked aspect in some cases is complicity. Many actresses might not have wanted to consent to sex but, on every threshold—including that of breaking into movies—a sacrifice is required. We know this instinctively.

One of the hardest truths to acknowledge about ourselves is complicity with our enemies. We bribe, we appease, we manipulate, we compromise. We don't hold fast. We don't stand. We don't put on the Armour of God and draw a line in the sand.

Let's remind ourselves of how serious complicity is when it comes to thresholds. Consider the mysterious episode in Scripture involving Moses, his wife Zipporah and his son Gershom. It happened as the family was travelling down to Egypt. Moses had been commissioned by God to confront Pharaoh and ask for the release of the children of Israel. He'd been extremely reluctant to make this journey. At least five times during his encounter with God at the burning bush, he'd effectively said, 'No! I won't do it. Pick someone else!'

Now God had offered Moses a name covenant at Mount Sinai—that is, a name exchange with covenantal blessings. He made His proposal by revealing a previously unknown name for Himself—I AM WHO I AM—and also suggesting to Moses a minor modification for his own name.[73]

This is all standard stuff when it comes to name covenant. Its three components are:

1. a name exchange, saying in effect, 'It's no longer "I" but "we".'
2. a revelation of a new divine name
3. a name tweak or replacement

However, there's a fourth aspect: a name covenant, significant as it is, is a prelude to a threshold covenant. There's no point in one without the other—the first is the gift of a new identity and destiny. The second is the invitation to pass through the doorway into that destiny. These two amazing offers are normally separated by six days in Scripture.

So, here's what happens when Moses leaves for Egypt. He's just repeatedly turned God down on the name covenant as well as the accompanying threshold covenant. Somewhere en route, he takes lodging. And there God tries to kill him.

This is an astounding and enigmatic incident: why would God commission Moses as His ambassador to Pharaoh and then, within just a few days, try to destroy him? It hardly makes sense. Yet there's a clue: the unusual Hebrew word for *lodging place*, 'malon', used in Exodus 4:24, seems to be a combination of 'maal', *act treacherously*, and 'lun', *lodging*.

And it's not the host of the inn who acted deviously; it was Moses. A threshold covenant in the spiritual is about passing over into your calling. A threshold covenant in the natural is about accepting hospitality and, in passing through the doorway, coming into covenant relationship with the host. This is completely unlike our modern way of doing things—it's not a simple monetary transaction. It's a covenant—a relationship whose primary purpose is 'oneness'.

Less than a week earlier God had offered this very same covenant to Moses at the burning bush and had been rejected. But now, spotting the 'House of Python' on the wilderness road, Moses was lured in by the food, wine and beds. In stepping over the threshold into the lodging, he acted treacherously—so this wasn't any ordinary wayside inn he'd entered. This shelter from the wind, sun and sand was probably a remote shrine to a desert god. And, in becoming one with that god, Moses would be tempted to bring the people out of Egypt to worship it, not the Lord of the Burning Bush. No wonder God acted so harshly. Moses was threatening to derail the Exodus before it even happened.

It was Zipporah who saved Moses' life. She remembered the 'sign' of the covenant. She remembered what Moses has forgotten. She remembered that El Shaddai—who has just revealed Himself as 'I AM'—long ago asked Abraham to circumcise all the males as a symbol of their dedication to Him. And she remembered that this hasn't happened for all the males in the room. So she took decisive action.

She performed a circumcision—whether it's on Moses himself or whether it's on Gershom is unclear. But with this reaffirmation of covenant, God ceased His attack. And Moses returned home. Where eventually Aaron found him.

Moses was given his name by the daughter of Pharaoh, who called him 'Moshe' because she said, 'I drew him out (*meshitihu*) of the water.' This relates his name to the verb 'mashah', meaning *to draw out*.[74] However, despite this Egyptian sense, his name also has a Hebrew sense related to 'mashiach', *the messiah, the anointed saviour* or *deliverer*. Yet despite this, it is Zipporah who does the rescuing in this instance.

In fact, she is the sixth woman—five of them mentioned by name in Exodus—who saves both his life and his mission. The woman who isn't mentioned by name is Pharaoh's daughter—perhaps because that would identify Pharaoh. And there's a point in mentioning the name of five women and not that of Pharaoh: because the greatest disaster that could befall a ruler of Egypt was to have their name blotted out of history.

Zipporah, צפרה, means *bird* or *sparrow*. This suggests the monstrous Ziz, the spirit of eclipses, was perceived as a giant 'zippor' or 'zipporah'. I've made a point of spelling out Zipporah's name in Hebrew, צפרה, because it starts with the letter 'tsadi'.

In this it is like another word that, at first sight, looks like the name of the spirit of forgetting: 'ziz'. However, this 'ziz' uses the letter 'tsadi' instead of the letter 'zayin'. It means *flower* or *curl* as in *lock of hair*, and it's related to Syriac words for *wing* and *feather*. And of course, 'ziz' with a 'tsadi' sounds remarkably similar to Ziz with a 'zayin'.

I need to repeat something here that I've said more than once before: God is not an etymologist—though He does not disdain that science. However, primarily He's a poet, a namesmith, a wordweaver.

Sometimes 'ziz' with a 'tsadi' is spelled 'tzitz', just to clarify that it isn't the same as 'ziz' with a 'zayin'. My apologies for all this emphasis on grammar and spelling, but I'm sure you've guessed there's something important hidden in the poetry of it all.

And if we fail to follow the poetry, we'll miss out on the nuances of what happens with Zipporah and how her name coupled with her words and actions are a prophecy of the Messiah. When Moses fails to remember the sign of the covenant and also fails to remember the consequences of breaking covenant, Zipporah 'covers' for him. Like a bird spreading its wings, she guards, shelters, protects, overshadows and atones for his failure through the sign of the covenant—circumcision—and the shedding of blood. 'You are a bridegroom of blood to me,' she says, prophesying of the Bridegroom-Messiah who will atone for the sins of the world. She's not just acting like the mother hen Jesus speaks of, protecting her chicks, but also like *hyssop*, ''ezob'. In a place of threshold covenant, she reminded her husband to learn from his mistakes. Her warning is for us too—but we've forgotten the dangers of a threshold and have no idea a covenant governs it. So her story seems simply brutal and disjointed.

Let's not miss the fact she's alert like a watchman, swift to act. So perhaps the flowers of memory—not just hyssop, since ''ezob' has a syllable rhyming with her name, but also myrrh and fennel, rose and almond—are sprinkled in the mix.

Her name is closely related to a modern Jewish one, invented from the Israeli national anthem, *Hatikvah*. 'Tzofiya' doesn't look much like 'Zipporah' in its transliterated English form, but a comparison of the Hebrew letters reveals their close connection. Tzofiya is spelled צופיה, while Zipporah is צפרה.[75]

Tzofiya means *she is watching*. It comes from the line in the *Hatikvah* which says: '*And towards the end of the East, an eye still watches over Zion*.'

Zipporah was a watcher. This is a common trait of many women in Scripture: Miriam, the sister of Moses, and of course the three Marys who were present at the crucifixion—Mary, the mother of Jesus, Mary, the wife of Cleopas, and Mary Magdalene. And although it could be expected of them, since their names are all variants of Mary—possibly coming from 'shomer', *watchtower*—there are some anonymous contenders for the role too.

Consider, for example, the woman of Samaria whom Jesus met at Sychar, near Jacob's Well. Now the apostle John could just as validly have commented that Jesus met the woman at Shechem. However 'Sychar' has different overtones and it hints that this is a threshold moment—both for Jesus and the woman. That is because the name of this village evokes the Hebrew for *threshold*, for *drink*, for *alcohol*, for *falsehood* and for *wages*.

Now Sychar was a neighbourhood of Shechem which, as already mentioned, was within Samaritan territory. Samaria itself means *watchtower* and Shechem means *shoulder*, indicative in Jewish culture of *government, keys* and *authority*. It's that ridge Jacob bequeathed to Joseph—an immensely significant location because there the kingship of the twelve tribes was ripped away from the House of David and government was wrenched from his line.

Ripping, tearing—threshold. If this doesn't remind you of Ziz, it should. Indeed, in later times, this city was ruled by Ahab and Jezebel—rulers who forgot truth, who worshipped false gods and who, through lying accusations, tore an inheritance from its rightful owner.

When Jesus went to Sychar, He went to mend history. He went to defeat Ziz by reminding the Samaritans of the truth. And He went to overcome another influential threshold spirit: Rachab, the spirit of wasting.

Nearly a thousand years previously, Rehoboam, grandson of David, went to Shechem to be proclaimed king. It's probable he went there because, back in those days, there was no spring of water in Jerusalem. That meant that one of the two requirements for a coronation—'living' water and anointing oil—was missing. The term 'living water' meant *flowing water* and Jerusalem simply didn't have any. The conversation of Jesus with the woman of Samaria about 'living water' has subtle undertones we miss: He was alluding to the kingship. That's why He went to

Sychar—to be proclaimed the Messiah by the Samaritans and restore a unified kingship to the line of David.

He went humbly, without a shred of arrogance. Because that was what had lost Rehoboam the kingship in the first place. Rehoboam had a name which actually includes 'Rachab', the spirit of wasting within it. The actual word 'rachab' means *to spread out, to broaden, to expand, to puff up, to be puffed up, to be arrogant.*

Rachab knows the adage, 'Pride goes before a fall,' from its Scriptural counterpart in Proverbs 16:18 far better than we do. It wants to tempt you to take on an attitude where it doesn't have to lift a finger to achieve anything. The spiritual legal consequences outlined in God's Word will take care of you. Because it can rely on the sowing-reaping principle to ensure your fall, it doesn't need to engineer the fall itself, just to produce circumstances where your deep-seated hidden pride will come to the surface and all you've worked to achieve will be undone in a single moment.

People who come out of the clutches of Python the constrictor are often initially relieved when things begin broadening out for them. But Rachab's agenda is to spread you so thin that all your efforts will be wasted. In military terms, it works to push you into territory where your supply lines can't reach you.

Rehoboam had a name, intended to be prophetic of territorial expansion and the spread of his rulership into new lands. Obviously he was given it in the hope that the kingdom of his father and grandfather would reach a new and dazzling zenith. Instead it all fell into ruins—right near Jacob's Well. When he came there to be anointed king and was asked to lighten the yoke that Solomon had put on the people, he replied: '*My father beat you with whips, but I will beat you with scorpions!*' (1 Kings 12:11 NLT) In his arrogance, he basically called up Leviathan, the spirit of backlash whose symbol is the scorpion. The retaliation wasn't long coming. It was so severe that Rehoboam lost the loyalty of ten of the twelve tribes. The kingdom split into north and south—with the remnant of the north eventually, in the time of Jesus, becoming Samaria.

To undo the work of Rachab, Leviathan and Ziz, Jesus visited Jacob's Well to restore what Rehoboam had lost. Jesus wanted to reunite the Davidic kingdom under one head. So he needed to find the person appointed to represent the place. From a spiritual perspective, the ideal person would have five covenantal relationships and a sixth dodgy pseudo-covenant. This is because Shechem, with a name symbolic of *government* and *authority*, had been the scene of five significant covenant re-affirmations in its history.

The first occurred when God appeared to Abram here. God had spoken to Abram previously but, at Shechem, He appeared for the first of three times. It was here, under an oak tree, Abram affirmed the relationship by building the first of seven altars.[76]

The second occurred when Jacob returned from his many years of servitude with Laban. Having wrestled with an angel, got a new name and been reconciled with Esau, he finally went to Shechem where he dug a well, built an altar and buried his household gods under an oak tree. That burial finally cut his ties with all but the

God of Abraham and Isaac. This is a re-affirmation of the covenant of his forebears.

The third and fourth ratifications of covenant occur during the time of Joshua. At the beginning of the occupation of the Promised Land and later, around the time just before his death, Joshua organised a ceremony to pronounce covenantal blessings and curses. He set up a memorial stone as a witness.

The fifth covenant is an evil one, but it is nevertheless legitimate. Abimelech, son of Gideon, was proclaimed king at Shechem. This was considerably before the time of Saul, widely regarded as Israel's first king. Abimelech's defiance of God, who was to be considered the only king of Israel, was clear-cut and deliberate. He killed all but one of his seventy brothers on a single stone—perhaps the witness memorial of Joshua. This is certainly a strong possibility, given the words of the surviving brother, Jotham, which directly reference Joshua's speech. Abimelech may well have been anointed king under the same oak as Abram built that first altar and Jacob buried his false gods. His defilement of this ancient site was so immense that Rehoboam was up against it from the start.

The sixth pseudo-covenant was that with Rehoboam's rival, Jeroboam—because it resulted in two kings at the same time.

So the woman of Samaria with her five marriages and her sixth de facto relationship was the perfect representative of Shechem. Jesus needed her to be at the right place at the right time in order to heal history, restore the land

and mend the world. When the Samaritans believe in Jesus and proclaim Him as the Messiah—the anointed one upon whose shoulder the government rests—they partake in that miraculous re-unification of a kingdom destroyed nearly a thousand years before.

It's not just the history of Shechem that Jesus had in His sights. He calls women—and men—everywhere to follow His example and take part in world-mending. To do so, He calls us, first of all, to remember. To remember the covenant in His blood, but also to remember His death and resurrection.

To remember that He is the Way, the Truth and the Life—and that no one comes to the Father except through Him. I know people who feel it's arrogant to believe that Jesus is the only way and that there are many paths to God. Personally—and without meaning any disrespect here—I think that it's an imperialistic insult to Islam and Buddhism, to Hinduism and neo-paganism, not to mention many animistic and tribal religions as well as New Age nature worship to suggest that all these modalities of spiritual expression are basically the same. To fail to recognise the individuality of all these faiths and to make-over other religions in the image of Christianity is a patronising, condescending offence to them all. And on the subject of individuality, only in Judaism and Christianity is there a loving Father Creator anyway.

And on the subject of dishonour, make no mistake about it, insulting the gods of another religion is a huge issue. As mentioned previously, it opens us to savage retaliation by Leviathan. We simply cannot dishonour anyone or anything.

Not even Jezebel. In many ways, especially not Jezebel.

The dealings of Jesus with the woman of Samaria, five-times-married-now-living-in-an-illicit-relationship, offer us the first hints of how He saw Jezebel of Samaria. Other hints can be found in His dealings with two anonymous females: the woman caught in adultery and the woman who'd suffered twelve years from an issue of blood.

This desperate woman had spent all her money on doctors and her last hope for a cure was Jesus. Unwilling to ask Him publicly for a miracle, she planned a surreptitious move: she would get close enough to touch the hem of His garment.

The prophecy of Malachi was explicit: '*For you who fear My name, the Sun of Righteousness will rise with healing in His wings.*' The 'wings' of a prayer shawl are the ends of the overgarment worn by orthodox Jews. Attached to these wings are tassels or fringes, known as 'tzitzit'. Let me spell that word out for you in Hebrew letters so the full implications become apparent: ציצית.

Yes, the first syllable is the 'ziz' with a 'tsadi' which means *flower*, *curl of hair* or *feather*, and which rhymes with the 'ziz' with a 'zayin' that describes the bird-like spirit of forgetting. These 'tzitzit' tassels attached to wings have a name related to *feather*. The poetic imagery is just exquisite.

No doubt this woman, as she planned her move, thought of the words in the scroll of Malachi. And also no doubt that particular Scriptural verse was commonly noised abroad as news spread of Jesus, and people '*begged Him to let the sick touch at least the fringe of His robe, and all who touched Him were healed.*' (Matthew 14:36 NLT) Perhaps it was those stories that emboldened her to think that, if she could just quietly, discreetly, inconspicuously be like those others, then the miraculous might descend into her life.

Her touch was feather-light but Jesus felt power move through Him as the woman fingered His direct access to the Father. The 'tzitzit' fringe symbolised Jesus' prayer life; each day as He slipped away to have time alone with His heavenly Father He would have handled the knots of the tassels in meditation and prayer.

Jesus forces her to testify to her healing, granting her recognition and respect. The early church historian Eusebius reported that she lived in Caesarea Philippi and that she had created a memorial to her gratitude which was still in existence nearly three centuries later: 'there stands upon an elevated stone, by the gates of her house, a brazen image of a woman kneeling, with her hands stretched out, as if she were praying. Opposite this is another upright image of a man, made of the same material, clothed decently in a double cloak, and extending his hand toward the woman. At his feet, beside the statue itself, is a certain strange plant, which climbs up to the hem of the brazen cloak, and is a remedy for all kinds of diseases. They say that this statue is an image of Jesus. It has remained to our day, so that we ourselves also saw it when we were staying in the city.'[77]

The threshold imagery is evident even here: the town is Caesarea Philippi where Jesus exchanges names with Simon[78] and makes His pronouncement about the gates of Hell; the statue of Jesus and the woman stands at the doorway, like a pair of threshold guardians; the herb that heals reminds us of the flowers and plants that aid memory and remembrance: rosemary, fennel, myrrh, rose of Sharon, almond, hyssop.

Remember, remember, remember.

> *'If you forget the Lord your God and go after other gods and serve them and worship them, I solemnly warn you today that you shall surely perish.'*
>
> Deuteronomy 8:19 ESV

The great medieval Jewish rabbi, Rashi, commented on this: 'If you have begun to forget, your end will be that you will forget *all*.'

Today, the upsurge in use of healing oils is a wonderful thing. Just as the upsurge in people wanting to create a culture of honour is. But we must never forget that human beings are incorrigible when it comes to idol-making. Oils all too easily become the source of health, not the God who gave us the plants to make the oils. Personally I love experimenting with essential oils and I have a theory there is a deep connection between them and the restoration of identity. Why else would God put the word 'shem', *name*, in 'shemen', *oil*?

And inspire someone to make a name covenant with it?

Many believers harbour a secret belief about their own inadequacy in prayer. They look around for the right words, the right formula, the right person. When they see God answering the prayers of other people, they sometimes decide, 'That's the person to pray for me.'

On occasion, this can mean travelling to another country to attend a specific church where that special person of faith is preaching or teaching. I have news: we are all inadequate. In fact, the first qualification for being used of God is inadequacy. And the second qualification is recognising it. It doesn't matter how much faith we have, it will never be enough. And it doesn't matter how small our faith is either. It can be as small as a mustard seed and still enough to move mountains.

The work of Christ is *finished* without a single second of effort from us.

It isn't *our* prayers that avail before the Father. It's *His* prayers—the intercessory pleas of Jesus—as He speaks on our behalf. So it's not about our perfect wording, achieving a higher level of faith for ourselves, seeking the right anointing, finding the right gifting or receiving ministry from that special person in the pulpit or on the stage.

No; it's about Jesus. All about Jesus. Never forget it's about Him—about the Master, not His servants.

Just as the woman who suffered from a blood flow for twelve years was healed by holding on to the prayer tassels on Jesus' tallit, so we need to hold on to His tzitzit too. By faith, we ask to touch the hem of His garment. We need to remember what we have forgotten; that we have a mediator and advocate in Jesus who we can ask to amend our prayers before they are presented to the Father.

It doesn't matter how pathetic or inadequate your prayer is—or alternatively how beautifully crafted it is—both are irrelevant. Because it's not about the wording, it's about the Word.

John's gospel is a literary masterpiece. Its design is exquisite—using matching themes, rather than a chronological approach. This is not to suggest that it is never sequential, because there definitely are occasions when it clearly states 'the next day', 'the following day' or 'three days later'. However, when it doesn't give a time reference, it is unwise to assume one. When theologians have presumed a linear progression of events in John's gospel then it follows that particular incidents were duplicated during His ministry. These include episodes like clearing the moneychangers out of the Temple and the invitation to dinner interrupted by a woman who anointed His feet with oil.

However, once it's obvious that the design is all about matching thematic episodes, it's a different story. Let's examine how the design works. Technically, John has used a favourite arrangement of Hebrew poetry called a 'chiasmus'—defined as a *rhetorical or literary device in which words, grammatical constructions, or concepts are repeated in reverse order*. In other words, he's made a pattern in his writing which works inwards from both back and front simultaneously. His gospel culminates in a central doublet with two 'I AM' statements and a shepherd motif. These two statements are: 'I AM the Good Shepherd' and 'I AM the Gate of the sheep.'

Now the following summary really only skates across the surface of the pattern. Each matching pair has deep links within the partners and also, in many cases, with the episodes on either side of them. John emphasises two aspects of the Christ in his presentation: the Shepherd and the Bridegroom.

His gospel starts with the Hymn to the Logos, consisting of 496 syllables and 17 words in the opening sentence. It ends with an account of 496 words and features the 17th triangular number, 153.

It records the testimony of a man named John, both front and back. At the start, John the Baptist speaks of the Lamb of God and, at the end, John the Apostle records Jesus' instructions about lambs and sheep.

Next the gospel tells of five disciples, including Simon Peter and Nathanael, who go after Jesus into Galilee. And, similarly positioned at the end, five groups of disciples, again including Simon Peter and Nathanael, head off after Jesus into Galilee. Nathanael is only ever mentioned in Scripture in these two places.

Embedded in the gathering of disciples for this first trip is a brief story about Nathanael having doubts. Matching this at the end is the episode of Thomas having doubts. This is one of the few places in the first half dozen pairs where the names don't match—however, if we assume the accuracy of the long Christian tradition that Bartholomew and Nathanael are the same person, then the match is very much closer: both Thomas and Bartholomew are derived from the name Ptolemy. Thus John seems to have included the Nathanael-has-doubts story, assuming that his readers knew Nathanael was also called Bartholomew, *son of Ptolemy*.

Moving on from these occasions, there are matching incidents with two women named Mary. At the beginning, the woman is Mary, mother of Jesus. At the end, it's Mary Magdalene. In both cases, the conversation is about bridal issues—at the start, it's about the provision of wine for the wedding feast at Cana and, at the end, the dialogue between Jesus and Mary Magdalene in the garden outside the tomb reflects the bridal scene in the *Song of Songs*.

Far be it from us, however, to deduce from this that Mary was married to Jesus—as many have done. Let's wait until the couplet of stories involving Nicodemus before we leap precipitously to this conclusion.

After this in John's narrative, the time sequence breaks down. Instead, the thematic pattern emerges more fully. The paired stories are Jesus overturning the tables of the money-changers and emptying the Temple with the account of the tomb being discovered empty. Because of the placement right after the Cana story, some scholars think that John's description of the ousted money-changers refers to an incident early in Jesus' career. They regard the story told by Matthew and Mark as describing a similar, but separate, and very much later event. However, John puts no time frame on the incident, whereas up to this point in his narrative his dating had been very clear. '*The next day*,' he says in both John 1:35 and 1:43 and '*on the third day*' in John 2:1. No such time-stamp appears on the story of emptying the Temple.

It's clear to me this incident did not happen twice. John describes one-and-the-same event as Matthew and Mark, however in my view he deliberately positioned it at the beginning of his gospel. His specific intention was to form a literary pair with the empty tomb. The thematic link between Temple and tomb would have been clear to his readers—they would have known a sacred shekel had an image of the god of death on it. The priestly hierarchy, prohibited from minting their own coins by the Romans, chose to get the highest quality silver from Tyre—and insisting the Temple tax could only be paid using these foreign-made shekels with a pagan god on them. The money-changers charged exorbitant fees to trade this offensive currency for ordinary coins. So John's point in matching these two scenes is: just as Jesus drove the god of death out of the Temple, so too He drove it out of the tomb.

The next set of paired stories in the line-up involve the Pharisee, Nicodemus. In the first episode, Jesus states it's necessary to be 'born again of water and the Spirit' and the meaning of this enigmatic phrase is only apparent in the parallel episode when Nicodemus is present at the crucifixion and sees the soldier pierce Jesus' side with a lance. Observing blood and water flow and knowing that the Greek word for 'blood' in this instance also means 'spirit', he would have realised that this was the moment of new birth. Just as the first Adam's bride, Eve, was born from his side, the Bride of Christ had just been birthed from the side of the Second Adam. This is why he brought so much myrrh to bury Jesus: it was the custom to anoint the Bridegroom.[79]

And then we're back to the two Johns. At the beginning, the Baptist is testifying of the Bridegroom and at the end the Apostle is testifying of the last words of Jesus: '*It is finished!*' In Hebrew, this is 'kalah' which also means *my bride* and has the overtones: 'It is consummated!'

The next set of story pairs involves Jesus meeting the Samaritan woman and Jesus before Pilate. At this point, the name matching breaks down and only the deep themes are in play. Both these stories feature truth, water and kingship. Indeed when it comes right down to it, they're about the proclamation of the true king.

And so the pairs go on and on. Until they hit a snag. And if there was going to be a hitch, there was one obvious place for it: the start of John chapter 8. This is the story of the woman caught in adultery. Some ancient manuscripts don't include this story at all; some include it, in whole or in part, after John 7:36, John 21:25, Luke 21:38 or Luke 24:53.

Ivan Panin pointed out that this is one of only two passages of any substantial length in the four gospels that are disputed. The earliest manuscript copies we have do not include the last twelve verses of Mark or this scene from John's gospel. Common to both the end of Mark and the story of the woman caught in adultery is God's grace to less-than-virtuous women. In the first, Mary Magdalene—notorious as the person who had seven demons cast out of her by Jesus—is honoured by being recorded as the first witness of the resurrection. In the second, a woman caught in the middle of a sexual liaison with a married man is presented to Jesus. Instead of condemning her, He writes in the sand, in some mysterious way shaming her accusers. Once they have left, He offers her forgiveness and a second chance.

Panin has noted that, at least in the case of Mark's gospel, while our earliest *copies* lack the last twelve verses, *even* earlier writings refer to them. He suggested that some copyist, like Uzzah who reached out his hand to steady the Ark of the Covenant, felt the need to 'right' the testimony of the apostles when it came to the place of women.[80]

Is there any way we can know where this story rightly goes? Luke or John? And, if John, does the patterning suggest a proper placement? I believe this story does indeed belong in John and that it's possible to know where it was first located. Instead of the beginning of chapter 8, I believe it should come at the end of that chapter—after the dispute between Jesus and the Pharisees about His identity.

If that happens, in my opinion all the paired episodes then align beautifully.

The story of the woman caught in adultery then matches Mary of Bethany anointing Jesus' head with oil and washing His feet with her tears. There's a very strong hint they are the same person. Or, if not, their sins are much the same. And that might suggest the removal of these two stories from early manuscripts was not about excising the role of women from the record but censoring the role of one particular woman: Mary Magdalene.

Yet that would be to defy a prophecy of Jesus.

Was Mary Magdalene the woman caught in adultery? John's literary structure is ambiguous—sometimes the episodes involve matching names; sometimes they don't. And sometimes the matching names belong to the same person, and sometimes they don't. But I personally believe they were the same person. And I think so for psychological reasons. You don't put yourself in a situation of shame—gate-crashing a social gathering and making a scandalous spectacle of yourself by crying all over the Guest and wiping His feet with your hair—unless you've been so excruciatingly shamed that you're totally beyond it.

Was Mary Magdalene also Mary of Bethany? Scholars may debate this issue but, in this case, I think the weight of evidence says 'yes'. Mary was the sister of Lazarus and Martha and she came from Bethany, but not—in my view—Magdala. It's my belief she was dubbed 'Magdalene' as a result of the name covenant she undertook with Jesus and that He gave her this famous name during their exchange.

Mary was an immoral woman, the 'Jezebel' of the gospels. Jesus had cast seven demons out of her. And, turning up at the house of Simon the Pharisee with an alabaster jar of spikenard, smelling of myrrh, she proceeded to plaster an incredibly costly and fragrant oil over Jesus.

Now 'myrrh' is fundamentally her name. The word for *oil*, 'shemen', is indivisible from *name*, 'shem'. This means that 'oil of myrrh' basically equals 'name of Mary'; and so she was splashing her name, identity and calling all over Jesus.

She was also covenanting. Delbert Hillers explains in *Covenant: The History of a Biblical Idea* that covenants could be forged using oil—as indicated by Hosea 12:1. He also points out they could be made using water, as demonstrated by Jeremiah 2:18. Now obviously these were unusual forms of the ceremony, but it clearly shows that what Mary did was not unprecedented.

The essence of covenant is oneness. Mary initiated a name covenant with Jesus, giving her name to Him through oil. She also gave it to Him through her tears since 'mar', is *weeping, crying* and 'mara'', *bitterness* or *salty water*.[81]

She used her hair. I hope you recall that a *lock of hair* is a 'ziz' (yes, the one with a 'tsadi', related to the 'tzitzit', *the prayer tassel*). Because forgetting and remembering is what this scene is all about: the forgiveness of sin and forgetting of the past; the remembrance of the present.

Now, for a true name covenant, names have to be exchanged. Mary not only had to give a name to Jesus but she had to receive one back. Preferably that name should be a subtle tweak of her own. Abram became Abraham and Sarai, Sarah; Saul became Paul; Phinchas became Phinehas; Gideon basically got a 'Gad' for the start of his name. Although Jacob looks like he got an entirely new name, it's likely he should never have been called *deceiver* to start with but always Israel, the male version of his grandmother's name, Sarah.

God's into playful poetry when it comes to names. So what does Jesus say about Mary? John doesn't record these words, but he doesn't need to. '*Truly I tell you, wherever this gospel is preached in all the world, what she has done will also be told in memory of her.'* (Matthew 26:13 BSB)

Memory. There's the name. The ultimate root of the many inter-related words for *memory* across European and Middle Eastern languages is said to be '(s)mer'. And the ultimate root of *watchtower*, and thus of *myrrh* and *Mary*, is thought to be '(sh)mar'.[82]

In this moment, with just a tiny finesse of pronunciation—though it's possible there wasn't even that because we simply don't know how Biblical Hebrew was pronounced—Jesus appointed Mary as *memory*. She would be the one, a week later, who was entrusted with the remembrance of what happened at the Resurrection. She became the 'Apostle to the Apostles' when she acted as the messenger who relayed the news of the empty tomb. And I imagine, for years afterwards, she corrected John and Peter about who exactly got *to* the tomb first versus who went *in* first.

Her calling was to become a mezuzah: the memorial and the watchtower. Not '**The** Mezuzah', because as we have seen, that was Jesus. But *a* mezuzah.

She was one of the watchers who stood guard at Jesus' death; she was the watcher who remained behind in the garden and encountered Him after He'd been raised from the dead. No wonder she was dubbed 'Magdalene'. It has a connotation of memory, memorial and remembrance and means *watchtower*.[83]

Mary Magdalene had been at the cross when Jesus said, 'It is finished!' This word in Aramaic also means *my bride*. Brian Simmons, in the Passion Translation, brings out this dual meaning by translating John 19:30 as '*It is finished, My bride!*'

It resonates with the power of '*It is done!*' as Jesus sits on His throne, saying: '*Behold I make all things new!*'

> *'It is done! I am the Alpha and the Omega, the beginning and the end. To the thirsty I will give from the spring of the water of life without payment.'*
>
> Revelation 21:6 ESV

In Greek, *done* is 'gegonan', *to come into being, to be born.*

Mary was probably still there when Nicodemus gasped, overcome with a sudden, mind-shattering revelation. As blood/spirit and water flowed from the pierced side of Jesus, he must have been awestruck, realising he'd just witnessed an event as momentous as the creation of Eve. A natural birth comes with the breaking of water and with blood, while the spiritual birth Jesus spoke of comes from water and the Spirit. The Bride of the Second Adam had to be born by faith from under His heart, just as the Bride of the First Adam was taken from the rib under his heart.

Nicodemus wasted no time as soon as he grasped the implications. For the consummation of a wedding, it was culturally necessary to have myrrh. In a staggering display of faith, he bought up a hundred *litra* of the oil of joy.

Less than a week before, Mary Magdalene had been accused of wasteful extravagance when she'd poured one *litra* of oil over Jesus. If Mary was reckless, how much more so was Nicodemus! The chances he had a hundred *litra* of myrrh—worth a million dollars in today's money—at home are next to nil. By spending the equivalent of one hundred years of wages for an ordinary labourer, he witnessed to the whole of Jerusalem through the oil-dealers: 'The Bridegroom of all creation is coming!'[84] (John 19:39)

When Mary and her friends took more spices to the tomb, Jerusalem was already abuzz with speculation: Nicodemus was either exceptionally eccentric or he had the inside story on *the* ultimate changepoint of history. *Myrrh*, after all, in Hebrew is spelled the same as *change*.

Mary, having wandered from her friends, was standing alone in the garden—a garden smelling of wafting myrrh and spices[85]—as the changes begin to avalanche. When Jesus mends history, He doesn't do it by halves. And He doesn't make an elaborate song-and-dance about it. He's quiet and unassuming.

The dialogue between Mary and Jesus captures so much in just a few words. First, it harks back to another garden—at the dawn of history. In Eden, God the gardener came looking for mankind asking, 'Where are you?' In the garden after the Resurrection, Mary as a representative of mankind came looking for God, asking, 'Where is He?'

Jesus was reversing Eden at that moment. God's words as He called to Adam allude to the severing of the oneness between humanity and Himself. Asking 'Where are you?' doesn't make sense unless the union has been ruptured.

But the scene in the garden outside the tomb shows that covenantal oneness has been made possible once more.

This reversal was only the beginning. Nicodemus had brought so much myrrh to the tomb that the whole neighbourhood would have been drenched in its aroma. The women had brought along spices as well. They brought them for a wedding, not a funeral. Along with Nicodemus, they were creating the 'mountains of spices' needed to fulfil the prophecy of the Bridegroom in the last two verses of the Song of Songs:

> *'O you who sit in the gardens,*
> *My companions are listening for your voice—*
> *Let me hear it!'*
>
> *'Hurry, my beloved,*
> *And be like a gazelle or a young stag*
> *On the mountains of spices.'*[86]
>
> Song of Songs 8:13–14 NAS

The word translated *gazelle* is the same word as *glory*, and that translated *stag* can also be *oak, ram, pillar, mighty man* or even, at not too great a stretch, *morning star*. Its meaning is simply *strong leader*, so its translation depends on context. Perhaps we could render it:

> *'Hurry, my beloved,*
> *And be glory, a strong leader*
> *On the mountains of spices.'*

A *strong leader*: a captain, the firstborn from the dead. In this evocative setting Mary asks the 'gardener' to tell her where Jesus is. *'They have taken my Lord away,' she said, 'and I don't know where they have put Him.'* (John 20:13 NIV)

Perhaps her words express oneness with Jesus through her name covenant. She probably used Aramaic מֹר, 'mori', for *my lord*. Also meaning *my master*, it has the same spelling as Hebrew *myrrh*, the base of her name.[86]

Her words echo the wedding scene in the Song of Songs when the friends of the Bride ask: *'Where has your beloved gone, O most beautiful among women? Where has your beloved turned, that we may seek Him with you?'* (Song of Songs 6:1 ESV)

As well as Eden reversed, this is the Marriage of the Lamb rehearsed![88] But other ancient echoes resound in this tiny sliver of conversation between Jesus and Mary. During their interaction, Canaanite religion is despoiled. Mary's words reflect the ritual involving Baal's return from the underworld. Each year, as winter ended and Baal's annual imprisonment came to an end, his worshippers would stand outside a cave and call, 'Where is the prince?'[89]

That question, 'Where is the prince?', was transformed into a name. A notorious name: Jezebel. The 'bel' element of her name comes from 'baal', *lord, master, husband*, so Jezebel is probably closer in meaning to 'Where is the lord?' with all its overtones of marriage.

Remember that Mary is 'the Magdalene', *watchtower*. Just as Jezebel is Queen of Samaria, *watchtower*.

With her words and name, Mary explicitly became a representative of the Samaritans and Canaanites. In fact—just so no one could in future argue that what Jesus did was for the Jewish people alone—she represented Jew, Gentile and Samaritan.

But she's not representative of the most noble of those races. She's representative of the worst. And she's a covenantal representative at that.

As the Bride of Christ, we are all Eve. Redeemed, surely, but still Eve. As the Bride of Christ, we are all Jezebel. Redeemed, surely, but still Jezebel.

When Jesus looks at those we accuse of being 'Jezebel', what He sees is the potential for a Mary Magdalene: an apostle to apostles.

To dishonour another believer is to dishonour the Bride. And to grieve the Bridegroom.

Prayer

Father God, I come to You in the name of Jesus. Yes, in His name, no other. By faith, I reach out into heavenly places and touch the hem of His garment, the tzitzit on His prayer shawl. I ask for access to His prayers before You.

I ask that You forgive me for all the times I've thought it's *my* faith You respond to, not His. I ask that You forgive me the times I've thought I've lacked the right level of faith to receive a response from You, when it's not about me. I forget at times that it's only and ever about Your only-begotten Son, Jesus of Nazareth. I ask that You forgive me the times I've had faith in faith, not faith in Him.

I recognise and repent of the many times I have rewarded myself with creature comforts instead of making You my first and only refuge. Whether the 'delicacy' has been food or not, whether it's been moral or immoral, it's still been my chosen way of forgetting the pain of the moment. It's been my way of consoling myself, apart from You. Through that 'delicacy', Lord, the spirit of forgetting has manoeuvred me ever further from You.

I renounce my 'delicacy', Lord, and the covenant I have made through it. I ask You to empower my repentance and, through the power of the Cross of Jesus, break that ungodly covenant.

I repent of failing to take responsibility for my decisions and for blaming others for the outcome. Forgive me. I repent of rebelling against You and then asking You to rescue me when I suddenly found myself in the enemy camp, surrounded and under attack. 'Where are You, Lord?' I wondered and I realise now I was basically asking that same question as that which forms Jezebel's name. Sometimes I called on Baal and the spirit of forgetting, and wondered why You didn't answer.

Father God, I speak to You now as the Abba of Jesus of Nazareth, both Saviour and Lord. I now make the conscious decision to renounce all agreement with Your enemy. I ask You to remove me from the entrapment Your adversary prepared for me. I am sorry, Father God, and I ask You to be my covering and shelter. I can only do this as I covenant with You and give You all the glory. I ask You to help me keep covenant with You.

Father God, I repent of the many times I just plain forgot or was too lazy to remember. Of the times I thought a decision or an event was not important enough to slot it firmly into my memory bank. Forgive me, Father God, for not honouring and treasuring Your precious gift to me—my memory. I ask You now to give me an awareness of what a wonderful gift it is and to protect it through Your sovereign power.

Father God, You appointed me a watchman. There have been many times I failed to be faithful in that aspect of my calling. I've turned away—turned a blind eye to situations and events that required a vigilant lookout and an alert warning to others. Forgive me, Father.

Forgive me, Father God, for the times I've been complicit with my family sins, iniquity and dysfunction. Cleanse me, Jesus with Your most precious blood of my pride and forgetfulness. Wash me with hyssop, and let others learn from my story. May Your deliverance of me resound to Your glory forevermore. And may You mend history through me, just as You did through Jesus.

In His name—holding on by faith to His tzitzit—and through the power of His precious blood. Amen

7

Through All Generations

It's easy to see how people got confused about Mary Magdalene and considered her to be the wife of Jesus. But as Arie Uittenbogaard points out, Nicodemus was making a statement as he 'unmistakably declared that the marriage of God and mankind had been consummated.'

God had tried once before. On Mount Sinai. There too the words of nuptial consummation—'it is finished'—had been pronounced.

> *'When Moses finished setting up the tabernacle, he anointed and consecrated it and all its furnishings. He also anointed and consecrated the altar and all its utensils.'*
>
> Numbers 7:1 NIV

Yechiel Eckstein comments on this verse: 'the word chosen by Scripture for *finished*, "kalot", can also mean *bride*. One reason for the allusion to a bride at this juncture in time is because the children of Israel were the bride and God the groom; the completed Tabernacle would be their shared home. However, there is another significance to this word with a double meaning. While "kalot" describes an ending, it also points to a beginning. A bride is a symbol of a new beginning as a woman begins a new life with her marriage. The word "kalot", with its opposite connotations, teaches us that every end is also a beginning.'[90]

Here in this verse describing Moses building the tabernacle at Sinai, we already have a foretaste of what it would mean for Jesus to finish His work of redemption and become the firstfruits of those to be resurrected.

Still, in case we missed this subtle allusion to the marriage covenant between God and His people at Sinai with its promise of new beginning, John seeded His gospel with other, more contemporary references. He clearly assumed his reader knew the stories of the birth of Jesus from the gospels of Matthew and Luke. Otherwise the external parallels—yes, not just internal parallelism but external too!—would have zoomed right over the reader's head and remain completely unnoticed.

There are only a very few places in the New Testament where myrrh is mentioned. One time is at the birth of Jesus when the magi brought gifts of gold, frankincense and myrrh. Almost all the other references belong to the week of His death—to the name covenant with Mary Magdalene or to the oil that Nicodemus brings to the tomb.[91]

But in connection with Nicodemus, John mentions Joseph of Arimathea—who parallels the Joseph present at the birth of Jesus—Joseph of Nazareth. Both Josephs were carers, tending to a helpless body, washed and wrapped in linen. They were helped by parallel sets of Marys—in the first instance, Joseph of Nazareth aided Mary, the mother of Jesus and, in the second instance, Joseph of Arimathea had the assistance of Mary Magdalene. In both situations there were angels, who announced: 'Don't be afraid.' In both cases, Jesus lay in a cave at night.[92] And outside, in the immediate neighbourhood, were watchers who were terrified by the angelic visitation. In the first case, the watchers were guarding sheep and in the second case, the watchers were guarding the Good Shepherd.

The birth from the virgin tomb uncannily reflects the birth from the virgin womb.[93]

John doesn't describe it; he relies on common knowledge but still he wants his readers to know that something new is happening. He wants them to realise that Jesus' word—'finished'—is both an ending and a beginning. It is a consummation, a marriage—it is God, the husband of Israel, completing His vows to His betrothed; it is the New Adam bringing forth His bride, the New Eve; it is the covenant of Sinai revisited, fulfilled, consummated.

It was when God offered this covenant that, according to many Jewish commentators, the faithfulness of women was most evident. They are understood to have been the first to agree to the Law; they are regarded as having no part in the incident with the golden calf; they are considered to have been the first to offer their jewellery for the adornment of the tabernacle. God even instructed Moses to speak to them gently, in contrast to the stern tone he was told to use with the men.[94] After the idolatry of the golden calf, the men of Israel lost a right that had been theirs since the beginning of time—the right to be priests in their own household. This privilege was handed over to the tribe of Levi because, when given a chance to side with God, they were the only ones who did.

When Jesus restored this right to the priesthood, He didn't give it back to just the wider body of men. He extended it to all believers.

The women at Sinai had a lot in common with the women at Golgotha: faithfulness, steadfast loyalty, sustained fidelity. Mary Magdalene epitomes those qualities, yet before she encountered Jesus, she was the poster girl for immorality. She had forgotten God but God had not forgotten her.

Mary Magdalene eventually became the face of 'memory' just as her counterpart, Jezebel, is the face of 'forgetting'.

One aspect of Christian community never ceases to amaze me: how many people have come into agreement with the spirit of Jezebel—Ziz—and forgotten what grace is. Torn apart the concept, in fact, then trampled the remains.

Imagine your life is represented by a house. Most lives are run-down, with gaping holes in walls, tumbledown brickwork, rotting fences, crumbling stairs. In short, a ruin. Now, into this house of your life comes Jesus. There He stands with the Holy Spirit and they consult together over the wreck. 'Can We cover this?' the Spirit asks. 'Yes, We can,' says Jesus.

Many believers have an idea of grace that pictures Jesus throwing a tarpaulin, stained with His blood, over the house so that His Father sees nothing. But I think that image trivialises His death, the power of His cross and the nature of grace to an appalling degree.

The word *cover* has more than one meaning in English. One of those meanings has migrated into the insurance sphere. There, to *cover* a house has the sense of providing the finances, resources and skill necessary to rebuild and restore it. To make it good as new, if not better.

Jesus doesn't want to present a Bride who is covered up, technically invisible to the Father's eyes, but a pile of rubble underneath. He wants to present a radiant, spotless Bride whose 'covering' has meant a rebuild and a scrubbing up so stupendous she is unrecognisable in her glory. I imagine Jesus, a huge smile on His face, presenting those who believe in Him to the Father: 'Okay, now, Abba—*who* is this dazzling creature? I'll give You three guesses.' And the Father, when faced with the splendour of what the blood of Jesus has been able to accomplish, will certainly remember our sins no more.

Grace does not mean we can simply ignore the law. Far from it.

Moses at Sinai said, 'Don't murder.' Jesus said, 'Don't even get angry, because that is murder of the heart.'

Moses at Sinai said, 'Don't commit adultery.' Jesus said, 'Don't even think a lustful thought, because that's adultery of the heart.'

Jesus didn't do away with the law of Moses by sidelining it, but by taking it to a new level. His commandment of love makes the law of Moses into a basic foundation. Jesus not only created a higher expectation for us, through His blood He empowered us to move into achieving it.

Grace isn't God turning a blind eye to sin. Grace is the power to overcome our personal failings as well as the iniquity of our generations. Grace is authority to mend the world. It's divine support to heal history. It's provision and sustenance to achieve our calling and, as part of that, to show the angelic principalities, powers and world rulers the manifold wisdom of God.

Grace is given to us so we can show Ziz and Python, Leviathan and Rachab—and many other angelic rulers—that the seeming foolish plans of God are incomparably wiser than any of their strategies or schemes. Even when the spirit of Jezebel influences us to forget, succeeding in tearing truth apart and squashing justice, God can still make a way through for us into His promises.

But the first thing we need to do is remember Him.

Remember God.

He has given us many practical steps.

> *Communion*: 'Do this in memory of Me.'
>
> *Mezuzah*: 'Write these commands on your doorposts: God is one. Love the Lord with all your heart and with all your soul and with all your strength.'

When it comes to thresholds, He exhorts us to take note of the dangers and follow His instructions explicitly. 'Remember Lot's wife,' He said, reminding us we need to be careful not to presume on grace.

We need to listen for His 'still, small voice', just as Elijah did. Elijah had fled from Jezebel. Somehow He forgot God. Even though he'd witnessed a spectacular answer to prayer and a demonstration of mighty fire-from-heaven, for some peculiar reason, he didn't think God would protect him. He'd eliminated 450 prophets of Baal and 400 priests of Asherah. However, somehow, Jezebel's threats caused him to forget God was in charge, not the queen of Samaria.

'*I alone am left*,' he says in 1 Kings 18:22 NAS. He'd forgotten the seven thousand people standing in solidarity with him as well as his support within the palace itself. Obadiah, the king's administrator, was a devout believer. He'd saved the lives of a hundred godly prophets, hiding and providing for them. And he'd reminded Elijah of this fact.

The defilement coming from Jezebel is like a cloak-of-forgetting. More than forty days later, having journeyed in the strength of angelic food and water to Mount Sinai,[95] Elijah still hadn't thrown off that mantle-of-forgetfulness. He still insisted to God he was the only one left. And despite hearing reassurances from God Himself, despite the heavenly sustenance and the defence from the wild elements of nature, he doesn't believe God will protect him. We can tell this because God gives him three people to anoint: Hazael as king of Aram, Jehu as king in Samaria and Elisha as Elijah's own successor. Of these, he only anoints the 'safe' one—Elisha. The dangerous men are anointed by other prophets.

When we forget God, it's not just truth that gets shredded. Trust goes too.

In lavishing His grace upon us, God asks us to remember Him, to partake of communion in memory of Him, to trust Him. He offers us His empowering favour to be greater than Elijah, greater than Moses, greater even than Jesus. '*Truly, truly, I tell you, whoever believes in Me will also do the works that I am doing. He will do even greater things than these, because I am going to the Father.*' (John 14:12 BSB)

This is what Jesus accomplished through His death, His resurrection and His visit to heaven on the first Easter Day. He went to the Father, continuing to follow the ancient blueprint He'd been given for the wedding and asking that His Bride be able to accomplish even more than He had.

> *'Hurry, my beloved,*
> *And be like a gazelle or a young stag*
> *On the mountains of spices.'*
>
> Song of Solomon 8:14 NAS

As previously pointed out, the word for *gazelle* can also be translated *glory*. It is צבי, 'tsebi' or 'tzebi', and can also be rendered *beauty* or *honour*. This bridal imagery links in with the prophecy of Isaiah:

> *No longer will they call you Deserted, or name your land Desolate. But you will be called Hephzibah, and your land Beulah; for the Lord will take delight in you, and your land will be married.*
>
> Isaiah 62:4 NIV

The poetry of these words isn't obvious in English: *deserted* is עזובה, 'azubah', *forsaken*. It is both a contrast and near-rhyme with חפציבה, 'hephzibah', *my delight is in her*. However חפציבה, 'hephzibah', also rhymes with צבי, 'tzebi', *glory, beauty, honour.*

In the previous chapter, Isaiah had prophesied a wedding instead of a funeral in his famous 'beauty for ashes' quote: '*To console those who mourn in Zion, to give them beauty for ashes, the oil of joy for mourning, the garment of praise for the spirit of heaviness; that they may be called trees of righteousness, the planting of the Lord, that He may be glorified.*'

The oil of joy—myrrh—the symbol of marriage replaces the mourning of a funeral. And in another delicate rhyme, *beauty* 'p'er' replaces *ashes*, 'epher'. Again the first casualty of translation is the poetry in God's words. The word for *trees* in the phrase 'trees of righteousness' is again 'ayil', which in Song of Songs was translated *stag* and which could be anything from *ram* to *pillar* to *morning star* to *strong leader* to *doorpost.*

Jesus is not just the Mezuzah, not just the Shemittah, not just the Chief Cornerstone, not just the Capstone, not just the Gate of the Sheep, not just the Key of Government but also the Bridegroom.

But He was also the 'suffering servant'—the One who, '*for the joy set before Him... endured the cross, scorning its shame, and sat down at the right hand of the throne of God.*' (Hebrews 12:2 NIV)

In the Garden of Gethsemane, *the oil press*, His Spirit was crushed for us. It was in that place that He agreed to drink the cup the Father set before Him and, in doing so, reached out through time and space to take on Himself the sins of the world. It was here that He identified with us in our pit of squalor, that He became one with us in an abyss so deep that we don't even know we should be ashamed of our pride and depravity because we've grown so used to luxuriating in them. He *became* our sin—an experience so devastating that He sweated drops of blood.

John Loren Sandford says: 'He became us, in order to reap as us, for us, on the cross we were due to reap. Praying as the God-Man, He identified with us, entered into us and became our sin.'[96]

It's not enough to see the potentiality for Mary Magdalene in those we accuse of being Jezebel. We have to recognise the Jezebel in ourselves. We have to enter Gethsemane by faith and watch with Jesus. We have to acknowledge our agreements with the spirit of forgetting, admit we've torn apart the truth, own up to the times we've ripped an inheritance and a calling out of the hands of others—sometimes by our actions and sometimes by our silence and inaction. We have to realise the Jezebels in our lives are ourselves.

John repeats the words of God to the church of Thyatira[97] in his vision of the return of Jesus:

> *'I have this against you, that you tolerate that woman Jezebel, who calls herself a prophetess and is teaching and seducing My servants to practice sexual immorality and to eat food sacrificed to idols. I gave her time to repent, but she refuses to repent of her sexual immorality. Behold, I will throw her onto a*

> *sickbed, and those who commit adultery with her I will throw into great tribulation, unless they repent of her works, and I will strike her children dead.'*
>
> Revelation 2:20–23 ESV

The last statement seems inordinately harsh. But again it returns us to the universal principle: we reap what we sow. The spirit of Jezebel sacrifices children to the god of Death; when this spirit is operating in us we cannot expect our own children to be safe. That applies to the spiritual 'child' we have to birth: our calling and destiny.

To go into Gethsemane and watch an hour with Jesus means to be willing to give up our self-righteousness, our condemnation of others, our isolation from the wider Body, our lovelessness.

Jesus has done everything necessary to overcome Ziz—that hellish spirit of Jezebel, of mutilation of truth, of immorality, of child sacrifice, of dispossession, of forgetting. He liberally pours out the oil of joy and surrounds us with songs of grace to ensure we can achieve this overcoming.

That grace He heaps on us is not an endorsement of sin. Neither is it toleration of sin. Grace is, in truth, God profoundly disagreeing with the way we live but giving us the power to change, anyway. All we have to do is ask.

Our prayers rarely come out of Gethsemane because we don't want the crushing involved: we don't want to be pressed out into oil for light. So our prayers tend to focus on our external circumstances. We'd rather have God change our situation than change us. We don't want to say with Jesus, '*...not My will, but Yours be done.*'[98] Or with Mary, '*...be it done to me according to Your word.*'[99]

When Mary spoke those words, she agreed to have the power of the most High overshadow her. In Scripture this word is often used on thresholds: it used to describe the guardian cherubim covering the mercy-seat—the place where heaven and earth touch in reconciliation; it is used to describe the cloud covering the Mount of Transfiguration—when the threshold covenant for the church was enacted; it is used in the song which outlines the conditions for protection on the threshold—Psalm 91.[100]

It's used to describe an assured and safeguarded pregnancy. Psalm 139:13 says: '*For You created my inmost being; You knit me together in my mother's womb.*' The Hebrew word for *knit together* is, in other contexts, translated as *overshadowed* or *woven.*[101]

It should be no surprise to find it hidden in one of those flowers that enhance memory. Solomon's bride—the Shulamite—in the Song of Songs gives herself the name, 'Ha'bazlith Sharon', *rose of Sharon*. The deeper resonances within this word, *rose*, suggests its inner meaning is *overshadowed by God's love*.

Jesus, the Rose of Sharon, offers us covenantal oneness so we can rest in the shadow of His wings—under His tallit, clinging to His prayers. We desperately need to be hidden from the power of the enemy at any threshold time: it's a critical and dangerous moment because Ziz is seeking to destroy all it can of our promised calling.

Just as Rosella blotted out the light, overshadowing the mother budgies, Ziz awaits its opportunity for a counterfeit overshadowing of our destiny through abortion, miscarriage or cot death. So to get to the place where God brings our destiny to birth and protects us as we start to crawl and toddle, we need to be in agreement with Him, not Ziz.

Our calling needs to be divinely overshadowed by love, knit together with joy, woven with gold.

And so, at last, we will become the Bride of prophecy:

> *...at your right hand is the royal bride in gold of Ophir.*
> *Listen, daughter, and pay careful attention:*
> *Forget your people and your father's house...*
> *All glorious is the princess within her chamber;*
> *her gown is interwoven with gold...*
> *Led in with joy and gladness,*
> *they enter the palace of the king...*
> *I will perpetuate your memory through all generations;*
> *therefore the nations will praise you for ever and ever.*
>
> Psalm 45:9–17 NIV

Prayer of PRAISE and THANKS

Father, I thank You for Your mercy and faithfulness, fresh and new every morning. I thank You for the gems and jewels of Your overshadowing love found in Your Word that are mine for the taking. I do not even have to ask—You have already made them available.

I thank You that You always remember me, and that You delight over me, singing with joy that I am part of Your bride. I thank You that You have re-*membered*, are re-*membering* and will re-*member* my heart and soul and mind and strength. I thank You for bringing me into covenantal oneness with You through the death of Jesus and His resurrection life. I thank You for healing the tearing apart of truth through forgetfulness, through false accusation, through disinheritance and through counterfeit covenant. Although I may not see the fullness of that healing today, I declare my trust in You. You are faithful, You keep Your promises, You will bring me into my inheritance in You, so that I may help in the rebuilding of Your Kingdom and the healing of history. May all of my thoughts, words and actions be a signpost to Your Kingdom of love in the world wherever I am.

Father, I praise and thank You that my spirit can again sing a love song to You for rescuing me from the pit of torn-apart truth. I sing of the wonders of who You really are—a God of forgiveness, mercy and compassion, slow to anger and abounding in love. Father, empower me with Your grace so that I can forgive, show mercy, offer compassion, be slow to anger and abound in love. Father, I thank You and praise You for Jesus making it possible for us to have that grace and to be one with You. I praise You that all the broken, ripped-up pieces of my life can come together to be as whole as that of Joseph, viceroy of Egypt, and as redeemed as that of Mary Magdalene, Your apostle, Your watchtower, Your keeper of memory.

Jesus, Lord and Christ, how can I thank You? What can I say to You? 'Thank You' for a gift beyond compare is so little. Thank You for keeping me close to Your heart when I ignored You. Thank You for pursuing me when I walked away. Thank You for bringing me back when I resisted every step of the way.

No one else can ever come near You when it comes to love and light, and grace and truth. You did this not just for me but for all humanity. I do not even know what to say to You except to say I will, through Your enabling grace, obey the words of the mezuzah: '*Hear, O Israel: The Lord our God, the Lord is one. Love the Lord your God with all your heart and with all your soul and with all your strength.*'

Amen

Appendix 1

Brief Summary

Ziz is a threshold spirit, mentioned several times in Scripture. Its name is found within the Hebrew word, 'mezuzah', *doorpost*. The doorpost was given a special place by command of God for memorial and remembrance.

Ziz was probably originally tasked with helping each of us to remember to love the Lord with all our heart, mind, soul and strength. As a fallen angel, it now presides over forgetting.

Throughout Scripture, there is a relationship between truth and remembering. The Greek word for *truth* means *not forgetting*. In English, the opposite of *re*membering is *dis*membering; this reveals a common theme in Biblical stories such as that of Joseph or Jezebel: forgetting is associated with the dismembering—or tearing apart—of truth. It can also be associated with false accusation.

Ziz has the same ultimate goal as Python but its modus operandi is completely different. Allied with Leviathan, the spirit of retaliation and backlash, Ziz tempts us to dishonour others, setting us up for reprisal. Like Leviathan, Ziz probably belongs to the class of angels known as seraphim. It is inadvisable to bind such spirits.

We are told by both Peter and Jude that anything beyond, 'The Lord rebuke you!' will land us in trouble. Actually abusing or reviling such spirits can be fatal.

These spirits actually want to tempt us to abuse or revile them—because then they don't have to exert themselves towards our downfall; they can just sit back and watch the Word of God take its course. They can rely on us reaping what we sowed; they can rely on a fall following pride; they can rely on dishonour of themselves—or any other part of God's creation—bringing deadly repercussions upon us.

However, they also know Jesus has stood in harm's way for us. All that we were due to reap was cancelled at the Cross—we need do nothing other than apply the finished work of Jesus. Their strategy is therefore immensely simple: encourage us to forget to turn to Jesus. Seduce us into such deep forgetting that we don't even think about repentance or forgiveness.

Ziz can be identified as the spirit of Jezebel. We can therefore be reassured that the spirit of forgetting can be overcome, and that those who refuse covenant with it and instead hold on to Jesus will be given authority over the nations.

We are called to discern the spirit of Jezebel and reject her teaching and renounce any covenant with her. However, we are also called to encourage those who follow this spirit towards the place where they become like Mary Magdalene. We are likewise called to discern the spirit of Ahab but to encourage those caught in its clutches to become like Joseph.

God has given us practical steps as well as good oils to help enhance memory. These include repetition of the 'first commandment' and such oils as rosemary, hyssop, fennel, almond, myrrh and rose of Sharon.

The spirit of Jezebel wants to rob us of inheritance, entice us into immorality and into ungodly covenants or to tempt us into a false refuge where we feast on a 'delicacy' of comfort away from God. This too is covenanting with another god. Since the nature of covenanting is oneness, this compromises any covenant with God. Once we realise we have another covenant, we should renounce it, asking Jesus to empower our words. Reliance on Jesus is a critical aspect of cutting off these issues since we only receive authority to deal with these angelic majesties once a godly threshold covenant is operational in our lives—the very thing Ziz is so keen to prevent.

Threshold covenants are not given at the same time as blood covenants, so caution regarding authority is always advisable.

To overcome Ziz, we simply need—having renounced all covenants and agreements—to stand firm and hold fast. We therefore need the armour of God which is specially designed for defence against spirits like Ziz and Leviathan.

We can ask God to restore to us all that Ziz has stolen, many times over. But we need to go asking, seeking and knocking on the door for this to happen. We can't just sit and wait for memory to return; we need to be active in pursuing it.

Ziz has some involvement with eclipses, with the 'shemittah', with laughter and with gold. All these 'signs' are ambiguous—sometimes they are positive and sometimes negative but they are not neutral. As signs from God that we should exert special caution, we need to consult closely with Him about their nature.

Ziz is a counterfeit of El Shaddai and of Jesus as the Mezuzah of God. It tries to undermine the importance of communion, which Jesus asked to be done in His memory. We receive help to overcome Ziz through giving thanks in all circumstances, thus building joy and strength.

Jesus is the Memorial, the Watchtower, the Name above all names. When we covenant with Him, He *knows* us and writes our names in His Book of Remembrance. In redeeming us, He treasures His Bride and overshadows us with His love.

We were once as ugly as an ashheap, full of all the dark corruption of Jezebel. However, by His grace He is transforming us into a Memorial to His name of exquisite and transcendent beauty.

Appendix 2

Common Symbols of Ziz

- griffin or other mythological bird such as a phoenix or benu
- feather, especially on a doorstep
- giant wings
- bird on a gatepost
- moving swarms
- bees humming 'zzzzzz'
- zzzzz's of sleep, lethargy (from 'lethe', *forget*) and the 'lotus-eaters' of Greek mythology
- eclipse
- gold
- mocking laughter
- a message box near a door hinge
- rosemary, hyssop, myrrh, fennel, almond, rose of Sharon
- watchtower, memorial tower, tower built for name or fame
- overshadowing in a deathly sense
- theft of inheritance
- false accusation
- anything that counterfeits communion
- lack of thankfulness, lack of expressed 'thank you'

Appendix 3

Governing Vows

It is very hard to reverse memory loss when a governing vow concerning memory is in operation.

In this context, a 'vow' is a statement of belief about life and how it will turn out, or about the worthiness of the self or a determined commitment to a particular goal. The vow may or may not be articulated verbally. Vows is generally acquired early in life and then forgotten—they become part of the background of our thoughts. We may speak them out every day and not notice them.

Vows acquire greater spiritual strength through the words *always* and *never*. Spirits do not make us vow but they can tempt us to do so and then empower our words towards fulfilment, thus reinforcing the original vow.

Typical negative vows are:

- people will always rip me off
- men will always harass me
- women will always manipulate me
- I'll never be a success
- our family will never get our rightful inheritance
- nothing ever goes right for me
- authority will always try to defraud me of my rights

All such vows interfere with God's call on our lives.

Getting rid of a vow is easy: just apply the finished work of Jesus at the cross to it. Repent of making it. Forgive those who tempted you to make it. Some vows will require you to withdraw your judgment of God and ask His forgiveness. Renounce the vow and ask for it to be cancelled at the Cross.

A 'governing vow' is, as its name implies, an overarching vow which may block the dismantling of other vows.

A vow such as 'I'm always right' will block repentance because 'repentance' by its very nature admits I'm *not* right. It doesn't necessarily block forgiveness because, if 'I'm always right', I'll certainly do the right thing and forgive.

A vow such as 'I'll never think of this ever again' will block repentance and forgiveness and therefore also block reconciliation and renunciation. It's the sort of vow Ziz loves to empower with forgetting because any incident traumatic enough to tempt someone to a vow like that is a timebomb ticking away. It's a governing vow—meaning there are a lot of little vows underneath it and none of them can be addressed because the overarching vow prevents it.

In the case of ritual abuse, the governing vow is generally 'I will never do anything to trigger the programming'—so unconditional forgiveness is often too risky in the person's mind. Just in case it triggers the programming. In this singular instance, triggers (also called seals) have to be removed before the vow can be taken down.

Appendix 4

Complicity and Salvation

One of the readers of the first draft of this manuscript asked a significant question: how does our complicity with spirits of the threshold like Ziz, Leviathan, Python or Rachab affect our salvation?

So that's why this appendix has been added in.

There are five specific kinds of covenants: they are blood, name, threshold (or cornerstone), salt and peace. Blood brotherhood ceremonies, such as those between David and Jonathan, use a combination of these. So too do marriage ceremonies. The 'covenant of freedom' mentioned in Jeremiah 34:8 and Jeremiah 34:15 is related to the shemittah and therefore appears to be a special type of threshold covenant.

There is a natural order to these five varieties of covenant: first, blood; second, name; third and fourth, threshold and salt; fifth, peace.

The blood covenant is all about salvation. Just as Abram was asleep when God undertook the blood covenant with him, so we too are asleep, dead in our sins, when God covenants with us in blood. It is all of Him, nothing of us.

We cannot add to our salvation, we cannot take away from it—this is the all-sufficient sacrifice of Christ on our behalf.

Complicity with these threshold spirits is going to make life absolutely unmanageable at times, but it's not going to take salvation from us. That blood covenant is a done deal, sealed in the Holy Spirit, untouchable.

However, thereafter it's a bit different. Name covenants and threshold covenants are not about salvation, they are about calling. They are about coming into the destiny and doing the good works that God has prepared for us to do, long before we were born. Now, once we have a blood covenant—the pledge of God for salvation—we're no longer dead in our sins. We're awake. We're called to be active participants in name and threshold covenants. To be part of a name exchange, for example, we've got to be a giver as well as a receiver.

At this point, complicity with such spirits means this: we are in basic agreement with the hosts of hell that one of their number has legitimate rights to our names and calling. We have not truly confessed with all our heart that every family in heaven and on earth, including ours, receives its name from the Father. (Ephesians 3:15) The Father is not going to honour us with a name covenant while we think that names aren't His. He's not going to honour us with a threshold covenant, if the first thing we're likely to do with one is to make a sacrifice of our calling to a god or goddess opposed to Him.

During the years we have a blood covenant with God but nothing else, our loyalty to Him is tested during times of spiritual warfare. We're not likely to be treacherous in times of peace. We don't suffer for our faithlessness—because Jesus took the penalty on Himself. But this is not going to be the case for other covenants; because we're 'awake' when we make them, both the blessings and the curses come our way. It is God's mercy, therefore, that He tests our loyalty before offering these additional covenants to us.

So, while our salvation is not at stake by complicity with fallen spirits, our calling, our destiny and our purpose is.

Appendix 5

Geography

God sometimes places His own mezuzot in the landscape. Places like Nebi Samwil, outside of Jerusalem, which the French Crusaders called *Montjoy*. And in my homeland of Australia: a hill called *Kurrkalnga*.

In 2009, I was checking on some finer points about indigenous tribal boundaries for a novel I'd been asked to edit. The detail was a minor one but I felt it was important to recognise the correct language group. As I searched the featureless red expanse on Google Earth, I felt an immensely strong impression to pray over a particular spot—an indistinct smudge in the back of nowhere. The nearest settlement was over twelve kilometres away as the crow flies. There was nothing to indicate the smudge marked any significant location. It had no label to identify it.

But for nearly a week, whenever I switched on the computer, I felt an urge to go to Google Earth and pray over what I started to call 'the flyspeck'. I didn't know its name, but I sure got to know its location: right near a t-junction where the track between Haasts Bluff and Kunparrka met the dirt road to Glen Helen. I'd been to Glen Helen and knew it was at the end of the bitumen, on the edge of the desert, about two hours west of Alice Springs.

Five years later, I saw a newsflash about a group of indigenous people who wanted to raise a Cross on an outback mountain. They were experiencing opposition from, of all people, other believers. It was an intriguing snippet and, as I looked deeper into it, I instantly recognised the location. It was my smudge at the t-junction—the flyspeck I'd prayed for! But now it had both an English name, 'Memory', and an aboriginal name, *Kurrkalnga.*

And because Google Earth had improved so much in the intervening years, I could get far more detail and I realised Memory Mountain had to be extremely close to the Tropic of Capricorn.

Now this Tropic forms a natural heavenly boundary: the sun never appears exactly overhead anywhere south of this line. As a boundary, it's a threshold and, if a memorial to God is sited on a threshold, it's basically a mezuzah. And just to confirm it—for me at least— *Kurrkalnga* on a map is a long thin shape just like a mezuzah and its latitude is 23° 25'12". The Tropic of Capricorn is, at present, 23° 26 '13.1" which, by simple subtraction, means that Memory Mountain is 1'1.1" inside the Tropic (or 1.01833 km).

Both 111 and 101 are significant numbers in Scripture: 111 is symbolic of covenant and 101 of sustenance and nurture. Yes! Of course: El Shaddai!

At the time of writing, the Cross is not yet constructed. But given those numbers, I don't doubt it will be.

But it makes me wonder. Where else in the world does God have His mezuzot?

Endnotes

1. Suggested by some scholars to be the same as Gilgal.

2. They demanded this explanation at Gilead—a territory on the east bank of the Jordan, divided between Gad, *troop*, and Manasseh, *forget*. I have to suspect that the idea of a memorial witness originated with the men of Manasseh, a tribe who would—because of their name—understand more than any others the dangers of forgetting and so wish to do everything they could to avoid it.

3. Lethe was the name of one of the five rivers of the Underworld in Greek mythology. All who died and came to the river drank of it and experienced complete forgetfulness of their former lives. It was also called the 'river of unmindfulness'. Lethargy is also an aspect of forgetfulness.

4. Arthur Burk in *Joy Unstoppable* makes the important observation that many modern translations, such as the NIV, say that *creatures* rather *people* feed on Leviathan. However he also points out that the Hebrew word, 'am', which comes up over a thousand times in Scripture is, in *every other* instance, translated *people*, not creatures.

5. It's incredibly tempting to suggest 'bees' here, even though there is a separate Hebrew word for bee, simply because bees hum that distinctive 'zzz' sound, which actually sounds like the name 'Ziz'.

6. Shadow bands during a total solar eclipse were described for the first time in *Völuspá*, a mythic poem from Iceland, regarded as being composed in the ninth century. Hermann Goldschmidt of Germany notes shadow bands in 1820 visible just before and after totality at some eclipses. George Airy, the English astronomer royal, saw his first total eclipse of the sun in 1842. He recalled shadow bands as one of the highlights: '*As the totality approached, a strange fluctuation of light was seen upon the walls and the ground, so striking that in some places children ran after it and tried to catch it with their hands.*'

7. http://www.etymonline.com/index.php?term=tefillin (accessed 30 September 2017)

8. https://en.wikipedia.org/wiki/Tefillin (accessed 30 September 2017)

9. Random House Dictionary © 2017 entry at http://www.dictionary.com/browse/phylactery

10. It's really necessary to have a good memory to be a gatekeeper. It's important to be able to recognise the names and faces of those with permission to enter or leave through the gateway; it's important to be able to identify the enemy at a distance and to distinguish friend from foe; it's important to be able to detect dubious documentation. So, for people called to be 'watchmen in the spirit', the most sustained and unremitting attack they will experience will be directed against their memory. It is the watchmen, the gatekeepers, who are called to the decisive conflict: to turn back the battle at the 'gates' before it reaches the 'city'.

    Part of their job is to point to the memorials of the past and to create memorials for generations to come. Just as the tribes of Gad, *troop*, and Manasseh, *forget*, and Reuben, *look! a son*, built *A Witness Between Us—that the Lord is God* so that their posterity would have a cairn that was a tangible point of reference to keep the memory intact.

11. In English, it is not immediately apparent that this is true: that Ziz is to be found within mezuzah. However, it's important to remember that ancient Hebrew had no vowels and that these came to be codified only about 1000 years ago. Thus the vowel 'i' in Ziz or 'u' in mezuzah cannot be taken into consideration. Only the consonants need to be considered.

12. See *Dealing with Python: Spirit of Constriction* in this same series.

13. First cousins once removed, or second cousins, depending on whether the Midianites were grandsons or great-grandsons of Abraham.

14. Also called the Ishmaelites, so there must have been inter-marriage between the children of Midian and those of Ishmael. Midian like Ishmael was a son of Abraham. With this double bond, the blood relationship to Joseph was quite strong.

15. Many people today seem to ignore the rhyming aspects of words in Scripture and look exclusively at the letters and how the meaning of the word can be understood from the letters comprising it. This is a really good way to analyse the depths of a word, providing the poetry is not discarded. There are many words in Hebrew with the same meaning which start with similar sounds but not the same letters. One such example is pertinent here. The words, 'zeph', 'kaph' and 'saph' all mean *pitch* as in a *covering of tar*. They rhyme quite nicely, but if you were

to analyse their meaning according to the functions of their letters, you would most likely conclude they were entirely different words.

16. Asenath may be Egyptian in origin, meaning *belonging to the goddess Neith*. However, it might also be a Canaanite name and refer to the war-like goddess Anat, the sister of Baal-Hadad. In this case Asenath would mean *holy to Anat*. Anat was often worshipped in Egypt during the Hyksos period and in some texts is actually identified with Neith. Zaphenath-Paneah has no known Egyptian etymology but is thought to mean *one to whom mysteries are revealed*.

17. Wikipedia shows a picture of the seal of Aperanat. Since Scripture records a signet ring (which would actually be the device that made the seal) as being given to Joseph, I wonder if the Petrie Museum in London has an item once actually touched by Joseph, son of Jacob.

18. The name Hyksos is believed to mean *rulers of the foreign countries*. These invaders conquered most of Egypt and ruled for about a century before being driven out. From their names and descriptions, they are believed to have been Canaanites. The Hyksos practised horse burials and horses seem to have been very important in their culture. Perhaps the mention of Joseph being given a chariot by Pharaoh alludes to this horse-loving culture.

19. http://newsfeed.time.com/2011/11/21/the-boundary-effect-entering-a-new-room-makes-you-forget-things/

20. Actually Leir, the legendary founder of Leicester, who is considered to be the same as the Welsh god Llyr and the Irish god Lir. Both of these are sea gods. Personally I think they are probably also the same as the Norse sea god Hler.

21. Mark Wolynn, *It Didn't Start With You: How Inherited Family Trauma Shapes Who We Are and How to End the Cycle*, Viking 2016

22. The medieval chronicle in question is Geoffrey of Monmouth's History of the Kings of Britain. While not always historically reliable, it is however an important resource when it comes to legend. And legend is all too often the repository of the spiritual aspects of the past. In Geoffrey's account, Leir is part of the dynasty of Brutus of Britain and he succeeded to the throne after his father Bladud died while attempting to fly with artificial wings. The dating is inexact, but Geoffrey made Bladud a contemporary of the biblical prophet Elijah. Leir was given the longest reign of Geoffrey's kings, ruling for sixty years. In Geoffrey's version of events, Leir asks his three daughters—Gonorilla, Regau and Cordeilla—which of them loves him the most. Gonorilla and Regau claim to do so extravagantly, but Leir's favourite and youngest daughter, Cordeilla simply says she loves him as a daughter should. She is immediately disinherited and exiled to Gaul, while the two flattering sisters get good husbands and half Leir's kingdom. However the two sisters conspire against their father and he is eventually forced to flee to Gaul himself. There he is reunited with Cordeilla who has married the king. Her husband raises an army and helps Leir defeats his enemies. King Leir once again takes possession of his lands around Leicester and reigns well for the next two years, until he dies. Cordeilla then buries her father under a temple dedicated to Janus. This has led some scholars to believe that Leir was essentially the equivalent of the Roman god, Janus. http://www.thiswasleicestershire.co.uk/2012/09/king-leir-of-leicester.html (accessed 24 December 2017)

23. 'One of the features of abuse is the fear you are losing your mind and that the things that have happened are figments of your imagination. Confusion sets in.' Anne M Gray, *Scared Silent by Shadows of the Past*, City Harvest 1999.

24. From the Dementia Australia website: 'Alzheimer's disease is the most common form of dementia, affecting up to 70% of all people with dementia. It was first recorded in 1907 by Dr Alois Alzheimer. Dr Alzheimer reported the case of Auguste Deter, a middle-aged woman with dementia and specific changes in her brain. For the next 60 years Alzheimer's disease was considered a rare condition that affected people under the age of 65. It was not until the 1970s that Dr Robert Katzman declared (rather boldly at the time) that "senile dementia" and Alzheimer's disease were the same condition and that neither were a normal part of aging.' https://www.dementia.org.au/about-dementia/types-of-dementia/alzheimers-disease (accessed 24 October 2017)

25. The geography of the dream was impeccable in its alignment with the real world. There really was a bridge just a few suburbs away that was 'the longest bridge in the world'—at least at the time. The Hornibrook Highway was a tollbridge that crossed a river mouth, linking Brighton with Redcliffe. It had a tower-like structure at each end. The pylons were very ordinary—however the bridge was a place where the mythic symbolism was speaking to anyone with spiritual sensitivity. When I started to talk to Maree (of the lost keys) about the spirit of forgetting, I naturally mentioned this dream about the 'longest bridge in the world' with its rainbow aspects. She asked me if the bridge quivered in my dreams. I had to say that I didn't recall it doing that. But, after she asked, I looked into other name meanings for this

mythic bridge: and yes, it is called the 'quivering road' or 'shaking way to heaven'. Maree wasn't the only colleague who had had childhood dreams about this bridge—so did several others. And one had dreamt of the tsunami as well. I came to the conclusion at this time (nearly forty years after the dreams themselves) that it wasn't simply about a mythic bridge out of European mythology, it was also about the indigenous songlines in landscape. Digging into the aboriginal legends of the past, it was clear there had been massive tsunamis along the nearby coastline—the story of the Glasshouse Mountains features a massive tidal wave. And in the nineteenth century, Stradbroke Island had been split in two by a giant tidal wave, cutting it into North Stradbroke and South Stradbroke, as it remains today.

26. I must, however, have sensed that was the language I needed to know. It was not only always the language I wanted to study, it was the language for which I bought dictionaries to facilitate that study. I've never got around to learning it—but I still have the dictionaries.

27. As for whether David Lake was correct in thinking that Lewis thought mankind to be the pinnacle of creation, I can do no better than quote from John Griffiths. In 1980, his survey of trends in British, American and Soviet science fiction was published. The way each nationality approached the genre was seen as so different to their counterparts in other lands that Griffiths titled his critical analysis, *Three Tomorrows*—to emphasise how diverse the future visions were.

    He pointed out that in the genre as a whole, there was an actual moment when mankind came to be seen differently: not as the pinnacle of evolution, but as just another creature in a multi-faceted universe. While American writers had never truly embraced this view as far as he could see, there was, as far as the rest of the world was concerned, an historical watershed after which it started to become the commonly accepted outlook. The book which made the most significant contribution towards the furtherance of this new and radical viewpoint was, in fact, by none other than C.S. Lewis. It was *Out of the Silent Planet.* Here is Griffith's view which, to my mind, comprehensively refutes Lake's assertion:

> *'...Lewis repeatedly tries to break his readers of the mental conditioning which makes them assume that superhuman intelligence must go hand in hand with monstrosity of form and ruthlessness of will. He tries, by using a cosmic scale, to put Man in what he thinks is Man's proper place, and deploys all sorts of tricks to do so.*
>
> *They were much shorter than any other animal he had seen on Malacandra, and he gathered that they were bipeds, though the lower limbs were so thick and sausage-like that he hesitated to call them legs. The bodies were a little narrower at the top than at the bottom so as to be very slightly pear-shaped, and the heads were neither round like those of the Hrossa, nor long like those of the Sorns, but almost square. They stumped along on narrow, heavy-looking feet which they seemed to press into the ground with unnecessary violence. And now their faces were becoming visible as masses of lumped and puckered flesh of variegated colour fringed in some*

> *bristly, dark substance... Suddenly with an indescribable change of feeling, he realised that he was looking at men.'*

John Griffiths, *Three Tomorrows: Aliens and Other Worlds*, The Macmillan Press Ltd, 1980

28. Just a few are Coventina, the Celtic goddess whose name means *disappearing memory* (amongst others); Munin, one of Odin's ravens, whose name is often rendered as *memory*; the Norse god, Mīmir, (from which our word 'memory' may come most directly) who guards the well of memory; Ganesha, the elephant-headed god of Hindu mythology because, after all, 'elephants never forget'. Although not directly related to memory words, I also include here a pair of threshold-related names: Janus, the Roman god of the doorway, and Aidan, *the sacred fire*. Originally the sacred fire was the family altar—the hearth. This altar was later moved to the threshold where the blood, painted on the lintels and doorposts, would drip into the shallow basin carved into the stone.

29. 'Every authority comes from God but not every authority is as God ordained it to be.' Anne M Gray, *Scared Silent by Shadows of the Past*, City Harvest 1999

30. Dr C. Edward Pitt in *Kintsukuroi Christians: Turning Mental Brokenness into Beauty* points out that the hippocampus is responsible for transforming working memory (short-term) into longer-term declarative memory. It is larger in children with autistic spectrum disorder than in children who develop more typically, as are the amygdalae.

31. 'If only' is an iconic regret associated with the activity of the spirit of Python. See *Dealing with Python: Spirit of Constriction*, the first book in this series.

32. This world of misted forgetfulness in *The Buried Giant* is evocative of Sheol, the realm of death in Hebrew conception. Sheol, *hell,* in Jewish thought has different overtones to the Greek underworld realms of Tartarus (a place of torment mentioned only in Scripture in 2 Peter 2:4) and of Hades (mentioned ten times in Scripture, including by Jesus when He speaks of the 'gates of hell' in Matthew 16:18). Sheol has perhaps overtones of the river Lethe of Greek mythology where the souls of the dead are required to drink the waters of forgetfulness and oblivion. The related Greek word, 'alétheia', *truth* or *not forgetting,* is used by Paul in his description of the Armour of God.

33. 'As the result of injury, emotional trauma, nutritional or other unresolved stress, the energy flow is interrupted, the whole body is affected. The exact nature of blockage in the energy flow can be more closely identified by 'muscle testing'... *Kinesiology is often called 'muscle balancing' or 'energy balancing'—helping the body into a better position to heal itself or reach a specified goal by harmonizing its energies.'* https://www.kinesiology.com.au/what-is-kinesiology-used-for (accessed 26 December 2017) Because the brain is not the repository of memory, but basically the 'filing cabinet' which records which body organ or muscle memory is stored in, kinesiology can, by muscle manipulation, remove the memory and disperse it through the body. It is not gone, it is dispersed—with the whole body taking the load one organ formerly did, it is possible to feel immensely better. However spiritual aspects of trauma are not dealt with this way—kinesiology is simply another form of false refuge, another consolation or comfort away from God. While it may be helpful in the short-term, the loss of the ability to retrieve a memory is not advisable in the long-term. Without a memory, it's impossible to know who or what to forgive.

34. http://www.ifcj.org/learn/holy-land-moments/daily-devotionals/holding-up-the-sky.html (accessed 1 November 2017)

35. Genesis 2:19–20 NAS: *'Out of the ground the Lord God formed every beast of the field and every bird of the sky, and brought them to the man to see what he would call them; and whatever the man called a living creature, that was its name. The man gave names to all the cattle, and to the birds of the sky, and to every beast of the field…'*

36. Genesis 1:1 and Ephesians 3:15. See *God's Pottery: The Sea of Names and the Pierced Inheritance* for further details.

37. God's words at Babel also reference the god of confusion, Bel the Confounder, as well as Marduk the scatterer, also called *the one who smites.*

38. From David Patterson, *Wrestling with the Angel: Towards a Jewish Understanding of the Nazi Assault on the Name,* Paragon House, 2006. Patterson was *commenting* on the thoughts of Rabbi Yaakov Culi.

39. http://shadowsofshoah.com/Survivor+Stories/Benjamin.html

40. Hitler's Cross: How the Cross was Used to Promote the Nazi Agenda, Erwin W Lutzer

41. Perhaps Elizabeth would have been originally considered in Hebrew to contain the syllable 'zeeb', *gold.* As I have repeatedly mentioned, the evocations of poetry were always of much deeper concern to God and His prophets than etymology. However, it should be noted that she is the mother of the forerunner, John the Baptist. As Zebedee is the father of the apostle John. Perhaps there is some significance in '*zab*eth' and '*zeb*ed' in relation to the Johns.

42. There were so many Levites in the time of Jesus that lots had to be drawn for the privilege of offering incense in the Temple. It was therefore a one-in-a-lifetime event and Zachary would never have had a second chance.

43. Jesus refers to the death of Zechariah in this rebuke of the Pharisees: '*Woe to you, scribes and Pharisees, hypocrites! For you build the tombs of the prophets and decorate the graves of the righteous, and you say, "If we had lived in the days of our ancestors, we would not have taken part with them in shedding the blood of the prophets." Thus you testify against yourselves that you are descendants of those who murdered the prophets. Fill up, then, the measure of your ancestors. You snakes, you brood of vipers! How can you escape being sentenced to hell? Therefore I send you prophets, sages, and scribes, some of whom you will kill and crucify, and some you will flog in your synagogues and pursue from town to town, so that upon you may come all the righteous blood shed on earth, from the blood of righteous Abel to the blood of Zechariah son of Barachiah, whom you murdered between the sanctuary and the altar. Truly I tell you, all this will come upon this generation.*' (Matthew 23:29–36 NRS)

44. That is, the original 1984 version of the NIV. Check out the next footnote to see what's happened in the 21st century.

45. There's no indication in the current NIV of 2011, apart from a note that the Hebrew is difficult to translate, that the former references to *mind* and *heart* have been substituted as follows: 'Who gives the *ibis* wisdom or gives the *rooster* understanding?' (Job 38:36 NIV) Here we seem to have a reference to Thoth—the ibis-headed god of the Egyptians—who was credited as the author of all works of science, religion, philosophy, and magic. The Greeks were a little more specific that the Egyptians, declaring Thoth

to be the inventor of astronomy, astrology, the science of numbers, mathematics, geometry, land surveying, medicine, botany, theology, civilized government, the alphabet, reading, writing, and oratory. They further claimed he was the true author of every work of every branch of knowledge, human and divine.

So, while 'ibis' is a good translator's choice for the mind as the 'seat of wisdom' symbolically and mythologically speaking, it's hardly a good fit for Hebrew thought.

The rooster is a motif of the Greek god of healing Asclepius. This deity also has a staff with entwined serpents which has become symbolic of today's medical profession. See *Dealing with Python: Spirit of Constriction*, the first book in this series for more detail. The rooster is also a bird of the threshold, since it crows at dawn—the boundary between night and day. While I think the translation of *rooster* in the latest version of the NIV leaves a lot to be desired, I nevertheless acknowledge that the *rooster*, because it's a bird that announces the threshold, is a suitable fit for 'sekviy' when it comes to Ziz, the sekwi.

46. Tom Hawkins of *Restoration in Christ* ministries was able to help many survivors of ritual abuse through his pioneering work in the practical applications of the 'Divine Council'. https://www.rcm-usa.org/index.html

47. Carthage was a Phoenician colony in what is now Tunisia. Allegedly founded by Dido (also called Elissa), the great-granddaughter of Ethbaal, it grew in power to be the only serious rival to the might of Rome in the long centuries of Rome's ascendancy. Carthage was said to be founded in the same century as Rome. (In the Latin version of Rome's founding, Romulus was said to be responsible; however, in the Greek version, the Trojan prince Aeneas became

the founder after fleeing the sack of Troy, visiting Dido in Carthage and finally making his way to the river Tiber in Italy.) The sacrifice of infants and children as an offering to the gods in Carthage (https://www.theguardian.com/science/2014/jan/21/carthaginians-sacrificed-own-children-study) is consistent with Biblical accounts of Moloch worship. Although until recently Greek, Roman and Hebrew stories of child sacrifice in Carthage and other Phoenician colonies were dismissed as propaganda against the enemy, this view while remaining contentious is being overturned by the finds of archaeology.

The Phoenician name for Moloch was Baal Melqart and the behaviour of his priests with their leaping and self-cutting rituals is similar to that described in the encounter of Elijah with the prophets of Baal. It can perhaps be assumed that these prophets were in fact priests of Baal Melqart. In later ages Melqart (or Moloch) was equated with the Greek Hercules—the 'Pillars of Hercules' separating the Atlantic Ocean from the Mediterranean Sea is a Greek description of the sea cliffs, however in a temple to Melqart near Cadiz were two eight-metre high bronze pillars proclaimed to be the true pillars of Hercules. The 'Pillars of Hercules' were commemorated in the original dollar symbol with its two vertical lines—the Phoenicians were the greatest sailors and traders of the ancient world, venturing where others feared to go. Although they did not invent coins, they were renowned for the high quality of their minted product.

48. Michael Youssef, *Discover the Power of One: make your life count*, FaithWords 2006

49. 1 Kings 18:9 and Genesis 47:22.

50. Tutankhamen, for example, married his half-sister, Ankhesenpaaten, who after his death is believed

to have married her grandfather. Tutankhamen's parents were also brother and sister. Father-daughter marriages also existed.

51. http://catchthefire.com.au/2016/08/204-queensland-babies-were-born-alive-during-abortions-then-left-to-die-health-minister/ (accessed 21 November 2017)

52. http://www.thepublicdiscourse.com/2017/09/20130/ (accessed 21 November 2017)

53. https://vimeo.com/159811104 (accessed 21 November 2017)

54. See *Dealing with Python: Spirit of Constriction*, the first book in this series.

55. The Hebrew word 'mittah' means *couch* or *bed*, and derives from 'natah', *bed, stretch, lie down, bow, incline, entice, turn away, leaning, lengthen*

56. Mount Hermon, which has now been dubbed the 'eyes of Israel' because of the military outpost there, watching for incursions from hostile neighbours.

57. For more information, check out Arie Uittenbogaard's comprehensive overview of the possibilities for the meaning of Samaria at http://www.abarim-publications.com/Meaning/Samaria.html#.WfwlzrURVdh

58. Rivka Sari, in her notes for the Torah Aromatherapy class, mentions this and also points out that 'shema' for *listening* may be involved in the word for *heavens*.

59. See Anne Hamilton, *God's Pageantry: The Threshold Guardians and the Covenant Defender*, Armour Books 2015, for more information on the flowers encoded into the Armour of God.

60. This meaning of *watcher* or *guardian* is even, curiously, found in Japanese. There, the name Mori is written in various ways but most often it has a character for *forest*, which denotes *the sacred grove around a Shinto shrine*. This same character is used to list the name in the Shinsen shojiroku which means *guard* or *keeper*.

61. http://www.telegraph.co.uk/gardening/grow-to-eat/rosemary-really-is-herb-of-remembrance-as-scent-boosts-memory-by/ (accessed 27 November 2017)

62. http://roberttisserand.com/2013/04/new-rosemary-memory-research/ (accessed 27 November 2017)

63. The medieval song, *Scarborough Faire*, preserves a connection between the herb rosemary and remembrance. This old variant also hints at thresholds with its mention of 'sycamore' and its request for an acre of land on the boundary of the land and sea.

Are you going to Scarborough Faire?
Parsley, sage, rosemary and thyme.
Remember me to one who lived there.
She once was a true love of mine.

Have her make me a cambric shirt.
Parsley, sage, rosemary and thyme.
Without no seams, nor fine needle work.
Then she'll be a true love of mine.

Tell her to weave it in a sycamore wood lane.
Parsley, sage, rosemary and thyme.
Gather it up in a basket of flowers.
Then she'll be a true love of mine.

Have her wash it in yonder dry well.
Parsley, sage, rosemary and thyme.

Where water ne'er sprung, nor drop of rain fell.
Then she'll be a true love of mine.

Tell her to find me an acre of land.
Parsley, sage, rosemary and thyme.
Between the sea foam and over the sand.
Then she'll be a true love of mine.

Plough the land with the horn of a lamb.
Parsley, sage, rosemary and thyme.
Then sow some seeds from north of the dam.
Then she'll be a true love of mine.

Have her reap it with a sickle of leather.
Parsley, sage, rosemary and thyme.
Gather it up in a bunch of heather.
Then she'll be a true love of mine.

If she tells me she can't, then I'll reply.
Parsley, sage, rosemary and thyme.
Let me know, that at least she will try.
Then she'll be a true love of mine.

Love imposes impossible tasks.
Parsley, sage, rosemary and thyme.
Though not more than any heart asks.
And I must know she's true love of mine.

When thou has finished thy task.
Parsley, sage, rosemary and thyme.
Come to me my hand for to ask.
For then you'll be a true love of mine.

64. The rose of Sharon is difficult to identify. It is sometimes considered to be cistus, *rock rose*, and sometimes to be the narcissus tazetta, known in Australia as the *jonquil*.

65. http://www.chaimbentorah.com/2013/12/word-study-hyssop/ (accessed 30 November 2017)

66. Perhaps we can see in this a reason for Jacob's prophecy over his son, Zebulon: '*...a haven for ships...*' A squadron of ships could, at a stretch, be categorised within the class of 'moving things'. It should be pointed out, however, while we're discussing Zebulon that Jacob's prophecy might not be what it seems. The territory allotted to Zebulon during the time of Joshua was basically land-locked. It may have had a tiny sliver of land that reached the sea but that's far from certain. Or it might have backed up to the lake that was the Sea of Galilee, but would that really qualify it as the '*haven for ships*' that was apparently prophesied here? Unless there's another nuance. And of course, there is. The town of Nazareth lies in the territory of Zebulon. Nazareth was the hidden haven for Jesus when His foster father Joseph returned with the family from Egypt after the death of Herod.

    In fact the Hebrew word for *ships* could also mean *mourning* or *time of lament*. But, taking it apart (and looking at it as two words rather than one), it could mean *the God who is I AM*. Imagine that. Long before God revealed His name *I AM* to Moses, Jacob prophesied that one day, the inheritance of Zebulun would be a haven for God Himself. But it's obvious why it would always be translated *ships*. Who could ever imagine God would need a haven?

67. http://www.letusreason.org/Pent5.htm (accessed 2 December 2017)

68. Although the obvious answer is Heimdall, because of the gold teeth, it might also involve Janus. In honour of Janus, people in Roman times celebrated the first of January with gift-giving—coins with the faces of Janus

were especially popular. Janus was also said to have a gold key which was said to open the 'celestial paradise'. (http://staffs.proboards.com/thread/3886 — accessed 30 November 2017)

69. Katheryn Pfisterer Darr in *Isaiah's Vision and the Family of God*, Westminster John Knox Press 1994, points out the rhyme involving 'azubah', *forsaken*, and 'hephzibah', *my delight is in her*. Nonetheless it should be noted that the rhyme is not exact: 'azubah' contains a zayin but 'hephzibah' contains a tsadi.

70. Some peculiar relationship exists between the words *leaning, mockery* and *death on a threshold*. In 2 Kings 7, an officer is with Joram, the son of Ahab and Jezebel, when the king goes to confront Elisha. The officer is never described by name but only as the man on whom the king was leaning (or alternatively, the Hebrew being ambiguous, as the one leaning on the king). He scoffs at the prophecy of Elisha about the raising of the siege of Samaria. Within a day, he is dead, having being trampled in the gate. The words *leaning*, the implication of *mockery*, and the *death in the gate of Samaria* are so reminiscent of similar words used in the lead-up to Jezebel's death that they seem deliberately chosen to evoke that previous event.

71. Job 41:5 ESV says: '*Will you play with him as with a bird, or will you put him on a leash for your girls?*' The word for *play* is in fact 'sahaq', *laugh*, which often occurs in relation to threshold moments: it is found when Abner and Joab decide to play a deadly threshold game in 2 Samuel 2:14 and it is found when the Philistines decide they'd like to have a laugh at Samson's expense but he brings down the house on top of them. The word for *bird* here is 'zipporah': perhaps this verse is a long-

lost subtle allusion to the alliance of Ziz and Leviathan, suggesting that we have no more chance of defeating one than the other. A few verses on there is also a command to *remember*: '*Lay your hands on him; remember the battle—you will not do it again!*' (Job 41:8 ESV)

72. Arthur Burk, *Joy Unstoppable*, Sapphire Leadership Group.

73. See *God's Priority*: *World-Mending and Generational Testing* for details. I believe that Moses consistently refused the name covenant God offered him; and that only by understanding the immensity of this offer can we understand the full extent of the treachery of Moses as he enters a lodging place on the way to Egypt. God's attack only makes sense in terms of desecration of covenant. The generational outworking of this refusal by Moses can be seen in the last few chapters of Judges.

74. As Wikipedia points out, this makes the Pharaoh's daughter's declaration a play on words. The princess made a grammatical mistake which is prophetic of his future role, as someone who will 'draw the people of Israel out of Egypt through the waters of the Red Sea.'

75. Remember to read the letters right to left.

76. http://www.dawntoduskpublications.com/html/oak_shechem_long.htm (accessed 6 December 2017)

77. http://www.newadvent.org/fathers/250107.htm (accessed 6 December 2017)

78. Jesus and Simon participate in a name covenant, which is the precursor to the threshold covenant that takes place six days later at the Transfiguration. This name covenant involves an exchange: Simon gives Jesus the

name 'Messiah', *the anointed one*, and Jesus gives Simon the name 'Cephas' *threshold stone* or *cornerstone*, for which the closest Greek equivalent was 'Petros', *the rock from which an enterprise is started*. 'Petros' has passed down to us in English as 'Peter' and we have been given the idea that these names are identical in meaning, but that is far from the case. 'Peter' could in fact be considered as closer to the Hebrew word 'peter', *firstborn, beginning, pioneer, one who opens the way*. Some believers cannot credit that Jesus would name Peter with the word *cornerstone*. Isn't Jesus the cornerstone? Yes, indeed, He is the Chief Cornerstone. It is through the oneness of covenant that Jesus, as the Chief Cornerstone, can exchange that part of that title of His and offer it to Simon.

79. http://www.abarim-publications.com/Meaning/Nicodemus.html#.WheosdKWZdg (accessed 7 December 2017)

80. Ivan Panin's magisterial mathematical analysis of these verses includes a comparison with the opening verses of the same gospel, showing both have the same 'numerical signature'.

81. Just about every descriptor of the scene involves Mary's name in some way. When we collect all the details in the three Gospel accounts of her pouring oil over Jesus' head and feet and consider the Hebrew words from which the Greek would have been translated, we discover the original depth of poetry hidden in the scene: mar, *crying*; mar, *drop, flowing down*; more, *myrrh*; merqach, *perfume*; merqachach, *pot of ointment*; mirzach, *banquet*; marach, *rub*; marat, *polish, plucked off hair*; margalah, *feet*; *at the place of the feet*; mara', *filthy*; mara', *lift up*; mara',

bitterness; mirmac, *trampling place*, mara'ashah, *at his head*; maruwq, *purification, bodily rubbing*; mirsha'ath, *wicked woman*; mirmah, *treachery, fraud*; mera', *mischief*; merea', *confidential friend*; mare' (Aramaic), *lord*; mori (Aramaic), *my lord*. All of these words are head rhymes for Mary. And all of them are either used in the text or alluded to indirectly.

82. To demonstrate the inter-relation of our modern word 'memory' with Samaria and with Mary, I can do no better than quote from the *Online Dictionary of Etymology* which lists the oldest common language root (shown here in bold):

    memory (noun): mid-13th century, *recollection (of someone or something)*; *awareness, consciousness*, also *fame, renown, reputation*, from Anglo-French 'memorie' (Old French 'memoire', 11th century, *mind, memory, remembrance*; *memorial, record*) and directly from Latin 'memoria', *memory, remembrance, faculty of remembering*, abstract noun from 'memor', *mindful, remembering*, from PIE [**proto-Indo-European language**] root ***(s)mer-** , *to remember* (Sanskrit 'smarati', *remembers*, Avestan 'mimara', *mindful*; Greek 'merimna', *care, thought*, 'mermeros', *causing anxiety, mischievous, baneful*; Serbo-Croatian 'mariti', *to care for*; Welsh 'marth', *sadness, anxiety*; Old Norse Mimir, name of the giant who guards the Well of Wisdom; Old English 'gemimor', *known*, 'murnan', *mourn, remember sorrowfully*; Dutch 'mijmeren', *to ponder*. Meaning *faculty of remembering* is late 14th century in English.

    (https://www.etymonline.com/word/memory — accessed 26 December 2017)

83. Magdalene, or of Magdala, comes from the Hebrew word, 'migdol', *watchtower*. This word contains an

element for 'twining', and is evocative of the knotted prayer tassels called 'tzitzit'.

84. Arie Uittenbogaard points out in the entry on Nicodemus at abarim-publications.com:

 'With his hundred *litre* of myrrh-oil (and a hundred is two times fifty, or a double witness to jubilee), Nicodemus unmistakably declared that the marriage of God and mankind had been consummated. He never went there to bury Christ; he went there to see Him be 'born again,' just as Jesus had explained him when the whole Nicodemus cycle started (John 3:3). The only other time that word σμυρνα (*smurna*) occurs in the gospels is in the nativity story, when the magi from the east gave it to Mary and Jesus when He was born the first time (Matthew 2:11).

 The older gospels had told the story of Christ's burial in Joseph's tomb but none of them mentioned Nicodemus' massive myrrh contribution (in Mark and Luke, the women bring spices; no myrrh is mentioned). It may have occurred to John that the audience of the older three gospels hadn't understood the resurrection as described by the earlier versions, and he may have inserted Nicodemus' outrageous gesture as a kind of inside joke. To people in the know, he couldn't have done it more obviously. A hundred *litra* of myrrh-oil. Custom of the Jews. A garden with a new tomb in which no one had yet laid, which is obvious to anyone a direct reference to the locked garden (the virgin bride) of the Song of Solomon 4:12 and the wafting spices of 4:16 (also see John 3:29).

 All gospels explain that Jesus' Body was placed in the tomb on the day before the Sabbath. And all gospels tell that the women went to the grave the day after Sabbath. Not a single member of a Jewish audience would have assumed that the women went to the tomb to embalm a person who'd been dead for two nights and a day (also see John's hint in John 11:31).

John goes through great lengths to explain that in reference to the resurrection, there are three kinds of people:

- People who don't want to hear about it, and who may or may not be aggressively opposed to discussing it.

- People who believe it on forehand (Nicodemus, Martha and probably the other women), who understand it as a general principle and who prepare for it.

- People who aren't opposed to it at all but who simply can't intellectually fathom it (mainly the disciples; see John 20:9)

Any gnostic or proto-gnostic in John's audience would have condemned the first and last group and worked hard to be in the second. But John shows that the resurrection occurs irrespective of people's beliefs and intellectual understanding. Even those who see the resurrection as a logical consequence of preceding Scriptures and events can not possibly predict the unimaginable practical manifestations of it. Even those who are violently opposed to it can experience it when it happens (Acts 9:5). But the most fertile group is composed of the people who are just ordinary folks, not the intellectuals but people whose beliefs are based on an everyday amicable interaction with Jesus. The resurrection does not occur by passing an exam; it occurs when it's time—and read for a closer look at the resurrection as a principle our article on the noun αναστασις (*anastasis*), from the verb ιστημι, (*histemi*).

John shows with great clarity that Nicodemus knew the resurrection to be precisely like someone's first birth; it happens when it happens and to whom it will happen. It can be predicted on forehand with the same kind of intellectual understanding that an unborn child has about its own birth and life on the outside. It happens because it's embedded in the way the universe works, and it doesn't happen due to our careful observations (Luke 17:20). God brings it about; He is the only active partner in the covenant He made with Abraham (Genesis 15:17, compare with Jeremiah 34:18), or in the words of Solomon: 'Lean not on your own understanding but trust in the Lord with all your heart.' (Proverbs 3:5).

The resurrection can be expected with an unwavering faith, but that faith isn't going to bring it about. If one's faith isn't based on a total surrender to the will of God, it will at best render the believer a front row seat to a spectacle he will not be part of.

85. The same combination, myrrh and spices, that is found in the description of Joseph's journey to Egypt with his cousins. This suggests Joseph's journey is to be understood as both a descent into death and a rebirth.

86. Actually, the nuances and translation choices here are quite stunning and varied:

    '*Hurry* (rhyming overtones of *eat, bless* and *create*) *my beloved,*

    And be .... (fill the space with your choice of: *gazelle, glory, honour, beauty*) *or* ……. (fill the space with your choice of: *stag, hart, ram, oak, pillar, doorpost, morning star, strong leader* + rhyming overtones of *drenched*)

On the mountains of spices.'

87. *Mori* is still used extensively by Yemenite Jews to designate a 'rabbi'.

88. John Bergsma at http://www.cuf.org/2014/01/wrote-book-love-comes-bridegroom/ (accessed 12 December 2017) notes:

    He is the divine bridegroom, the one promised in the prophets (Hosea 2:14–23). In fact, John the Baptist identifies Him as such: 'The one who has the bride is the bridegroom; the best man, who stands and listens for him, rejoices at the bridegroom's voice.' (John 3:29).

    Just a few verses later, Jesus travels through Samaria and meets the famous Samaritan 'woman at the well' (John 4). We need to remember that the patriarchs Isaac, Jacob, and Moses all met their wives at a well (Genesis 24:10–27; 29:9–14; Exodus 2:16–22). In fact, Jesus sits down at 'Jacob's well' (John 4:6) where Jacob met Rachel (according to tradition). So we expect some sort of betrothal scene. As Jesus and the woman talk, the topic of marriage does come up explicitly: 'You have had five husbands, and the one you are with now is not your husband.' (John 4:18) Jesus goes on to reveal Himself to the woman as the Messiah (John 4:25–26), whom Jews held to be the bridegroom of the Song of Songs. The woman is astounded and walks into her town testifying to this great prophet. As a result, the town 'converts' to Jesus (John 4:40–42). Jesus has 'wooed' this entire town to Himself, beginning with this woman with a checkered past.

The bridegroom images continue. In John 12:1–7, at the beginning of His Passion Week, Mary anoints Jesus at Bethany with 'pure nard'. Nard is only mentioned in one Old Testament book: the Song of Songs, where it is a wedding perfume on the bodies of Solomon and his bride (Song 1:12; 4:13,14). Interestingly, Jesus connects this wedding perfume with His death: 'Let her keep [the rest of] this for my burial.' (John 12:7).

And so it's at Jesus' death where the next several bridegroom images pop up. At the cross, they crown Jesus (with thorns) just as an ancient Israelite groom was crowned on his wedding day (John 19:2; Song 3:10). They remove His clothing, as a bridegroom does when approaching the bridal chamber (John 19:23). At the moment of death, He asks for a drink of (soured) wine, reminding us of the cup of wine that ends the Jewish wedding ceremony (John 19:28). He drinks and says, 'It is consummated,' which has marital connotations in the original language of the Gospel (Greek), as it does in English. Joseph of Arimathea and Nicodemus take Jesus down and anoint His body with 'myrrh and aloes', a combination of spices only mentioned in marital contexts in the Bible! (Psalm 45:8; Proverbs 7:17; Song 4:14) They place His body in a tomb 'in which no one had ever been laid' (John 19:41), that is, in a virginal tomb—just as he entered the world in a virginal womb.

To cap it all off, on the morning of His Resurrection, Mary Magdalene runs to the tomb while it is still the dark of night. She looks for Jesus but does not find Him. She encounters some angels, whom Jews called 'the watchmen of heaven'. She asks them about Jesus, but then immediately turns to discover the Lord.

89. Because this is a religious ritual, the question, 'Where...?' implies *concealment*.

90. Yechiel Eckstein, *Holy Land Moments Daily Devotional*, 'Every End is a New Beginning', 25 May 2015 This agrees with the creation account: '*Thus the heavens and the earth were finished, and all the host of them.*' (Genesis 2:1 KJV) The word *finished* in the original Hebrew indicates an action completed in the past, never to occur again. It is related to 'kalah', *married, betrothed* with the sense of *consummation*: the climax of one state which as it ends heralds a new beginning.

91. The single exception is in Revelation 18:13 where myrrh is mentioned in the lament over Babylon. It is one of the cargoes that, because of the fall of Babylon, can no longer be sold for profit by traders.

92. Rev. Sarah McGregor on Facebook commented on my post on this topic: 'This comment came in from one of my followers: 'Also at the birth he is laid in a "phatne", a Greek word meaning *a niche*, that is, probably a hollow scraped into the interior wall of a first century house, because there was no room in the "kataluma", which means not *inn* but *living room*. Jesus eats the Last Supper in a "kataluma", the only other time it is mentioned in the New Testament.'

93. Or, as Rebekah on my Facebook page commented with this provocative thought: 'So ... Jesus was ... born again. Because He had become a man, and unless a man be born again, He (even He!) cannot see the Kingdom of God?'

94. See *More Precious than Pearls: The Mother's Blessing and God's Favour Towards Women*, Anne Hamilton and Natalie Tensen, Armour Books 2016

95. Mount Horeb is the same as Mount Sinai. The word 'horeb' is basically the same as 'cherub', indicating it is the mountain of angels. However, 'horeb' means *sword.* Sinai is a difficult word—sometimes it said to come from the moon god, Sin, or at others to mean *muddy* or *hostility* or *thorn*. Jones' Dictionary of Old Testament Proper Names renders it: *bush of the Lord.*

96. John Loren Sandford, Paula Sandford, Lee Bowman, *Choosing Forgiveness: Turning from Guilt, Bitterness and Resentment Towards a Life of Wholeness and Peace,* Charisma Media 2013

97. Thyatira is said to mean *sacrifice* though, as a Greek word, the most obvious meaning is *castle of Thya*. An alternative—*sacrifice offering*—was suggested by Hitchcock's *New and Complete Analysis of the Holy Bible* and by Arnold Fruchtenbaum in *Footsteps of the Messiah.*

98. Luke 22:42 NIV

99. Luke 1:38 NAS

100. In fact *overshadowing* occurs right after the verse which mentions protection from the 'fowler's snare'. '*Surely He will save you from the fowler's snare and from the deadly pestilence. He will cover you with his feathers, and under his wings you will find refuge.*' (Psalm 91:3–4 NIV) Perhaps this 'fowler's snare' or 'bird trap' alludes to Ziz. Certainly Python is mentioned in verse 13, which also alludes to Leviathan. This entire psalm proclaims God's protection on the threshold and the conditions for obtaining His covenantal defence. Many Christian believers today think of it as unconditionally promising God's covering. However, if we still retain our 'false refuges', we invalidate the tremendous divine assurances given there.

The implications of the satan quoting verse 13 on the threshold of Jesus' ministry are explored extensively in *Dealing with Python: Spirit of Constriction*, the first book in this series.

101. The word for *overshadow*, 'sakak', is related to cakak, *cover* and is translated as *weaving* when describing a child in a womb. The rose of Sharon is, in my view, a daffodil–like plant with a yellow trumpet and creamy petals: the narcissus tazetta.

CPSIA information can be obtained
at www.ICGtesting.com
Printed in the USA
LVHW041807240623
750448LV00003B/126

9 781925 380125